The Grit Cookbook

World-Wise, Down-Home Recipes

by Jessica Greene and Ted Hafer

CHICAGO
REVIEW
PRESS

Library of Congress Cataloging-in-Publication Data
Greene, Jessica
  The Grit Cookbook / by Jessica Greene and Ted Hafer.
    p.   cm. —
  Includes index.
  ISBN-10: 1-55652-648-2
  ISBN-13: 978-1-55652-648-0
  1. Vegetarian cookery. 2. Grit (Restaurant) I. Hafer, Ted. II. Title. III. Chicago Review Press.
TX837.G6743 2001
641.5'636—dc21   2001051460

The recipes in this book require careful preparation as well as the use of proper ingredients. Neither the author nor the publisher assumes any liability for the preparation and/or consumption of food prepared using the recipes included in this book.

Cover and interior design: Anne Richmond Boston
Interior art: Edward Hafer
Center photograph on back jacket contains an image of an untitled drawing by Michael Lachowski.
© 2001 by Michael Lachowski. Used with permission.

This revised and updated edition published by
Chicago Review Press, Incorporated
814 North Franklin Street
Chicago, Illinois 60610
ISBN-13: 978-1-55652-648-0
ISBN-10: 1-55652-648-2
Printed in the United States of America
5 4 3 2 1

Happy 20th Birthday to the Grit!

This revised edition of *The Grit Cookbook* heralds the 20th anniversary of the existence of The Grit with over 20 new recipes for soups, sauces, dressings, desserts, and main courses. A new wave of creativity has swept through our kitchen since the first edition, and the next generation of Grit chefs has transcribed a sample of their latest meatless wizardry for you. (Please see Acknowledgments, page 177.) We've included more quotes from friends and fans, and also a special glimpse of the very birth of The Grit (even before our day!) in the words of founders Jennifer Hartley and Melanie Haner Reynolds.

So take your thoughts back to the beginning while bringing your taste buds right up to the minute, and enjoy the 20th anniversary edition of *The Grit Cookbook.*

—Ted Hafer and Jessica Greene

For Jack and Paulina

"The Golden Bowl. I had tasted, but never actually ordered, the notorious Golden Bowl until I worked at The Grit. I order mine with broccoli and cheese. If I feel ambitious (or if I have had a bad day), I add a side of yeast gravy to the mix. It is quite a treat to sit on your couch, watch a movie (or bad TV) and eat a Golden Bowl from the Asian to-go boxes they are packed in. Oh, and it has to be accompanied by a sweet tea."

—AMY DYKES,
I AM THE WORLD TRADE CENTER

"If I could bathe in the Golden Bowl, I would . . . the greatest invention *ever*!"

—DJ HAMMOND, JE SUIS FRANCE

contents

the founders of the grit speak

The Grit had a name way before it had an existence. I remember telling my friends (or anyone who would listen), "I'm gonna open a coffeehouse/art gallery and it's gonna be called The Grit." "Cool" or a disinterested "really . . . ?" was the common response, then "Why The Grit?" My answer: "No reason, I just like the sound of it." It's Southern, like grits, and humble, like a single molecule or a speck of something. So there you have it. Fortunately, The Grit has surpassed its humble, southern speck of a beginning to become what it is today.

—JENNIFER HARTLEY, GRIT FOUNDER

The Grit was born one day when Jennifer Hartley and I were eating lunch at The Gyro Wrap around March of 1986 and talking about our dream jobs. We ended up down at the Station because Jennifer had already decided it was the ideal place to open our gallery/café, and were approached by the owner-of-the-moment of T. K. Hardy's, offering us the end storefront with the cool rolling metal warehouse door for $300 a month. Somehow we actually managed to open for business in October of that year, with thanks to our third partner Peggy Cozart, her father, Jennifer's mother, and lots of friends willing to dance to K.C. and the Sunshine Band 45s while climbing ridiculously tall scaffolding to paint and hang our own version of track lighting.

Things were a lot different back then. Some of the most memorable times were art openings when we might actually make over $200 a night, largely in the sale of longneck Buds; the lighting of Andy Nasisse's sculpture/pyre on the patio; Deonna Mann, Joey Tatum et al. performing on scaffolding INSIDE the restaurant in their band Crack (probably our biggest night); Michael Stipe ending his writer's block and writing the lyrics for "Welcome to the Occupation" while sitting in the loft sipping coffee one fall afternoon; the subsequent filming of the dance sequence for "The One I Love" video; Folk Music and Dance Society's hoot night, where Vic Chestnutt was known to contribute a song or two after several shots of espresso; and, mostly, conversation of the most useless yet memorable sort, largely orchestrated in slow Southern twang by John and Sam Seawright, Armistead Welford, or any other of the numerous poetic and artistic visitors to our wonderful little world. I stayed with The Grit until around February 1988. Jennifer ran the place on her own for around a year or more (with the help of her future husband John Rogers) until Jessica and Brenda Roberson took over, turning it into more of a restaurant; i.e., they actually had an oven. Exit Brenda a little while later, enter Jenna Smith and Sue Hoagland (later of Guaranteed fame). Sue exits at some point, Ted enters, and the rest, as they say, is history. My husband, Tom Reynolds (whom I met when he was doing some repair work at the old Grit in exchange for meals), and I actually attended the opening of the new location on our wedding night, May 12, 1990. (Contrary to its at times questionable reputation, The Grit has always been a hotbed of matrimonial bliss.) I'm sure I've made mistakes myself in the telling of it, but I'm proud of my Grit past (my relatives, to their astonishment I'm sure, will all be getting copies of the cookbook for Christmas). We made lifelong friends in that little kitchen. I'm glad to see it continuing in such fine hands as Ted and Jessica's, and hope it will go on and on. Maybe like the Varsity. An alternative, tattooed version of it.

—MELANIE HANER REYNOLDS, GRIT FOUNDER

introduction

Early on at The Grit, things were somewhat lean. When the restaurant was young in the 1990s, many people didn't want to give it a try, for fear that vegetarian food would prove to be freaky health food. And there it was, in that old brick building with peeling paint, not really near anything else, in a part of our hometown of Athens, Georgia, that was a red-light district at night. *Yikes!*

Now The Grit is surrounded by thriving businesses. It's filled with happy throngs of people who know they'll get a big delicious meal that just happens to be without meat. They know we're not food snobs or health police.

Only a small portion of our customers are totally vegetarian. Many of them know they can be bad at The Grit. (How about **Mac and Cheese**, **Deep Dark Chocolate Cake**, and **Vanilla Iced Coffee** for lunch?) But they all know they can get freshly prepared, simple, wholesome food in generous servings.

Continually surprising people with how good vegetarian food can be keeps things fun, but often the surprise is ours. The level of customers' devotion, the reach of The Grit's reputation, the degree to which travelers and Athens expatriates tell us they yearn for Grit food, and the constant requests for a cookbook—all this continually surprises us. The Grit is small and humble, never much for blowing its own horn, but people keep showing their love and it makes us proud.

Of course, horn blowing takes a back seat to guitar thrashing around here. The Grit owes much of its personality to its association with the many varied forms of rock music. From the 95 percent-plus staff who have been or are in bands to the man who owns the building, musically talented and/or obsessed people have helped shape The Grit since its beginning. For better or worse, that's who we are, and our friends and fans in the music world have been very generous with their support and accolades for Grit food. That's Athens for you!

But let's talk about food. Our food is not timidly seasoned. We love garlic, onions, vinegar, and lots of other ingredients that give food a kick. That's also what our customers love. But it only works because it's balanced. Central to successful seasoning is salt—the demonized mineral that is often not associated with vegetarian cooking. It's dubbed the Governor of Flavor at The Grit, and salt's pivotal role in cooking is as deeply acknowledged here as its health risks are exaggerated elsewhere. Vegetarian food's bland reputation rests largely on salt phobia. But do not fear, Grit customers and cookbook readers, we are not salt mongers. We use it, but we don't abuse it.

In any case, we welcome you to adjust any and all seasonings herein to your own liking. By all means, taste these dishes as you make them and engage in any bastardizations you deem necessary. After all, some garlic is very hot and some is not, and we know from our own kitchen experience that not all measuring spoons are created equal.

Generally, these recipes have plentiful yields compared to some cookbooks. We guess that if you are bothering to cook from scratch, you may want to share with others, enjoy multiple meals, or even freeze portions for later consumption.

To make vegans' lives a little easier, we've noted all of our dairy-free vegetarian recipes with the Ⓥ throughout.

Whip up several items at once and play Grit if you like. The freedom and spontaneity of The Grit kitchen spawned these tasty concoctions (and also made it difficult to choose what to include!). So share in the spirit that resides in the cool old building at 199 Prince Avenue and let good food bring you joy.

pantry prerequisites

Here's a handy list of items from the supermarket or natural food store that bear mention because we use them very frequently or strongly prefer a certain variety or brand—or just because they're downright unusual. Keep in your refrigerator and pantry:

- **Salted butter**
- **Vegan margarine (no whey, baby!)**
- **Light brown sugar**
- **Vegan Worcestershire sauce (many cheap store brands are anchovy-free)**
- **Brewed dark soy sauce**
- **Firm tofu**
- **Dry mustard**
- **White pepper**
- **Balsamic vinegar**
- **Heinz cider vinegar**
- **Heinz ketchup**
- **Crystal or Frank's hot sauce**
- **Morningstar Farms breakfast link vegetarian "sausage"**
- **Morningstar Farms Recipe Crumbles (ground beef substitute)**

- Nutritional yeast (an inactive yeast with a cheesy taste that makes it a must for tofu dishes)
- Tempeh (a soy product nutritionally more complex than tofu and equally versatile)
- T.V.P. (textured vegetable protein, in chicken and beef flavors)
- Semisweet chocolate chips
- High-butterfat (22 to 24 percent), unsweetened cocoa powder

The good news for everybody except those fellas who sued Oprah is that most supermarkets now carry lots of items for the meatless cuisine buff that until recently were only available at natural food stores. *Yee-haw!*

fundamentals

The Grit has always served generous portions of food because we want satisfied customers. The same goes for this cookbook. With so many people over the years telling us they wish they could cook like The Grit does, we've decided to serve up the recipes people want, provide generous yields, and really show them the ropes.

Since some recipes are the secret ingredients for others, a batch of this might call for a batch of that. That's why we have this section called "Fundamentals." Take our beloved Grit Yeast Gravy as an example. It's the secret ingredient for **Grit Collard Greens** and **Chicken Salad-Style Tofu**, as well a habit-forming way to smother our **Golden Bowl**, **Garlic-Parsley Mashed Potatoes**, and **Grit Brunch Biscuits Deluxe**.

We've kept these links to a minimum, but a true Grit cookbook wouldn't be complete without these (mostly vegan) essentials. The fundamentals always appear in color.

- **Grit Black Bean Chili**
- **Grit Pintos**
- **Grit Salsa**
- **Grit Marinara**
- **Grit Yeast Gravy**
- **Grit-Style Tofu**
- **Grit Indian Spice**

"I haven't been to Athens since 2001. I was telling everyone we have to go to the amazing monosyllabic restaurant. Peyton said 'Grit.' I said 'That's it, let's not be too late!'"

—BOB NASTANOVICH, PAVEMENT/SILVER JEWS

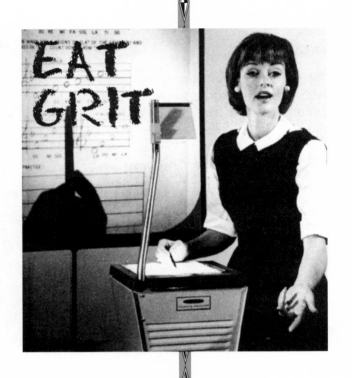

"I have had many obsessions in my life, but none so overwhelming as my obsession with Grit Tofu. Over the years I lived in Athens, I spent days trying to perfect that taste and that texture in my own kitchen. But nothing has worked, so I finally gave up and accepted that only a chosen few will ever know the secret recipe. That way, every Sunday brunch I end up drooling in anticipation while I wait—and it's more fun that way."

—KITTY SNYDER

"The Grit, besides simply being one of the finer enjoyments of life, is easily my greatest weapon to convince my more carnivorous friends that vegetarian food can be delicious. If I had a dozen or so disciples, I think that's what would be served at our last meal."

—BRIAN TEASLEY, MAN OR ASTRO-MAN?

Grit Black Bean Chili Ⓥ

Years of pleading for this recipe can now cease. Slap this stuff on chips and cover with melted cheese for some fine nachos. Save the rest for a **Mondo Burrito**, **Breakfast Burrito**, or **Black Bean Staple**. This is a large batch, so there's plenty to enjoy. This chili also freezes well.

1 quart dried black beans, sorted and rinsed
Water to soak and cook beans
1 medium yellow onion, finely chopped
2 tablespoons minced fresh garlic
3 tablespoons dark chili powder
2 teaspoons cumin powder
2 tablespoons fresh oregano or 2 teaspoons dried
1 teaspoon cayenne pepper
1/2 teaspoon freshly ground black pepper

1 small or 1/2 large green bell pepper, finely chopped
1/3 to 1/2 bunch celery, with leaves removed and finely chopped
1/2 small or 1/4 large yellow onion, minced
Vegetable oil
1 cup fresh or frozen corn
1 cup shredded carrots
2 (28-ounce) cans crushed tomatoes
2/3 cup #3 bulgur wheat
1 tablespoon plus 2 teaspoons salt

fundamentals

Soak beans overnight, or for at least 6 hours, in water to cover (or boil beans for 2 minutes in water to cover and set aside, covered, to soak for 2 hours).

Drain and rinse beans and place in large cooking pot with finely chopped medium onion, garlic, and dry spices. Add enough water to cover, plus 1-1/2 inches. Bring to a simmer, stirring occasionally, until beans are very tender, 1 hour or more. If necessary, add water in small increments to avoid burning and maintain simmer.

As beans cook, sauté green pepper, celery, and remaining onion in a small amount of vegetable oil until they are translucent and celery is tender.

When beans are done and still very hot, combine all ingredients in a large bowl or pot and blend well. Allow flavors to marry for at least 1 hour. Serve hot or enjoy reheated later.

Yields 16 servings.

fundamentals

Grit Pintos V

A simple, delicious essential for the mighty **Pasta Fagiole**, or the beloved **Grit Staple**—our pintos over steamed brown rice topped with sautéed vegetables of choice, minced red onion, and a generous amount of shredded cheese.

1 quart dried pinto beans, sorted and rinsed	1 scant tablespoon cumin powder
Water to soak and cook beans	1 tablespoon plus 1 teaspoon salt
1 small or 1/2 large yellow onion, finely chopped	1 teaspoon freshly ground black pepper
2 tablespoons minced fresh garlic	Additional water as necessary

Soak beans overnight, or for at least 6 hours, in water to cover (or boil beans for 2 minutes in water to cover and set aside, covered, to soak 2 hours).

   Drain and rinse beans and combine with all other ingredients except salt in a large cooking pot. Add enough water to cover, plus 1-1/2 inches. Bring to a full boil, loosely covered. Reduce to a simmer, stirring occasionally, until beans are very tender, 1 hour or more. If necessary, add water in small increments to avoid burning and maintain simmer. When beans are tender, add salt and stir well.

Yields approximately 12 cups.

Grit Salsa

For dipping chips or jazzing up brunch dishes, burritos, guacamole, or Spanish rice, here's a big bowl of our famous Grit Salsa.

- 1/2 ripe medium tomato (or 1 small Roma tomato), chopped
- 1 (28-ounce) can diced tomatoes
- Juice of 1/2 lemon
- Leaves of 4 to 5 fresh cilantro stems
- 1 medium clove fresh garlic, chopped
- 1 small jalapeño chile (or more to taste), chopped
- 1/3 medium red onion, chopped
- 2 tablespoons cider vinegar
- 1/4 teaspoon cumin powder
- 1/2 teaspoon dark chili powder
- 1/2 teaspoon freshly ground black pepper
- 1/2 teaspoon salt

In food processor, grind tomatoes and lemon juice on pulse setting just until very finely chopped but not pureed. Place in large mixing bowl.

Place cilantro leaves, garlic, and jalapeño in food processor and grind thoroughly. Add chopped onion and grind on pulse setting just until very finely minced. Combine all ingredients in mixing bowl, stir together well. Serve immediately or cover and refrigerate until fully chilled.

Yields 4 cups.

fundamentals

"I've never been one to let my canines go to waste, but The Grit brings out the herbivore in me! The Loaded Nachos make me feel like Popeye on a spinach binge."

—JON CROXTON,
THE WEE TURTLES

fundamentals

Grit Marinara Ⓥ

A big batch, but hey, want to make a great lasagna? Paired with Grit Pintos for **Pasta Fagiole** or on a simple pita pizza, this sauce is simple and delicious.

3 tablespoons extra-virgin olive oil
1/2 medium yellow onion, finely
    chopped
2 tablespoons minced fresh garlic
1 tablespoon finely chopped fresh
    parsley or 1 scant teaspoon dried
1 scant tablespoon fresh oregano or
    1 scant teaspoon dried
1 tablespoon finely chopped fresh
    basil or 1 scant teaspoon dried

1-1/2 teaspoon salt
1-1/2 teaspoon sugar
1/2 generous teaspoon freshly
    ground black pepper
2/3 cup of water
1 teaspoon freshly squeezed lemon
    juice
2 (28-ounce) cans crushed tomatoes

In a large, heavy-bottom saucepan, heat oil over medium-high heat. Add onion and garlic and sauté until onions are translucent and garlic is well sizzled, approximately 5 minutes. Add remaining ingredients and stir often until mixture just begins to bubble. Lower heat and simmer for 20 minutes, stirring frequently.

Yields approximately 8 cups.

"I sometimes order the pita pizza, and every time I do, someone will say, 'Man, I didn't know they have pizza here?!' I have taken many a guest there, from bands like the All American Rejects to folks like David Cross, Patton Oswalt, Paul Rudd, and Oprah's favorite author, Greg Behrendt."

—CHRIS BILHEIMER, KRUSH GIRLS

Grit Yeast Gravy V

Truly a Grit favorite, our yeast gravy instills profound cravings among devotees who are denied it even briefly. People dig it! It lends its stunningly un-vegetarian flavor to fellow Grit dishes such as our **Collard Greens** and **Chicken Salad-Style Tofu.** This recipe is easily halved.

- 1 cup (2 sticks) vegan margarine
- 3/4 cup whole wheat flour
- 3/4 cup flaked nutritional yeast
- 2 cups regular (not reduced-fat) soy milk
- 1/2 cup soy sauce
- 1-3/4 cup hot water
- 2 tablespoons vegan Worcestershire sauce

In a large, heavy-bottom saucepan over medium heat, melt margarine completely. Stir in flour and yeast until blended and continue to heat roux until mixture begins to bubble. Use only enough heat to maintain vigorous bubbling, whisking constantly for 4 minutes. This is the time required to cook the flour to smoothness, and vigorous whisking is important to avoid burning.

   Continue rapid, thorough whisking and add soy milk gradually. The mixture will quickly become thick and custard-like. Combine soy sauce, water, and Worcestershire sauce and add to gravy gradually. Blend well after every addition and do not add liquid so rapidly that gravy is very thin. If gravy does become too thin from the addition of too much liquid, continued cooking will thicken it.

Yields 4 cups.

"Oh, for an ocean of Grit Yeast Gravy."
—DOTTIE ALEXANDER, OF MONTREAL

fundamentals

"There's yeast gravy all over our yeast gravy page."
—JOHN SHARPE, FORMER ATHENIAN HALL-OF-FAMER

fundamentals

"The reason I love The
Grit? One can't do better
than the Golden Bowl, the
old stand-by. Yes, add the
veggies, add the cheese.
It's culinary nirvana."

—BILL MALLONEE,
VIGILANTES OF LOVE

Grit-Style Tofu Ⓥ

When cooked correctly, tofu can be reminiscent of succulent fried chicken. The secret is to get the water out and the flavor in. The Grit's method is to cook it twice. The essentials are a non-stick skillet, soy sauce, and nutritional yeast.

One of the restaurant's favorites is our **Golden Bowl**—Grit-Style Tofu served over steamed brown rice drizzled with melted butter (or vegan margarine), topped with Grit Yeast Gravy or sautéed vegetables and shredded mild cheddar.

    1 (15-ounce) block firm tofu
    Vegetable oil
    Soy sauce
    Nutritional yeast

Cut tofu into cubes slightly smaller than playing dice. Lightly oil a non-stick skillet and place over high heat. Allow oil to heat slightly and add tofu. Sauté, tossing with a non-metal spatula until evenly and lightly golden brown. Sprinkle lightly with soy sauce, sauté briefly to further brown tofu. Remove from skillet, draining and discarding any excess fluid.

Rinse and wipe skillet dry, lightly oil, and place it over high heat. Allow oil to become very hot and add tofu. Sauté tofu, tossing with a non-metal spatula almost constantly until very well browned. Sprinkle with soy sauce to taste. Sprinkle with nutritional yeast to coat tofu cubes and, tossing vigorously, sauté for a few seconds and remove from heat. Serve immediately.

Personal tastes with regard to salty soy sauce flavor and amount of nutritional yeast "breading" vary widely. Excessive soy sauce will make the tofu too salty, while too much oil and yeast will give a gooey result. At its best, this recipe yields tofu with a slightly crispy, deliciously yeasty exterior and a tender, moist interior.

Yields 2 servings.

Grit Indian Spice V

The foundation of Indian cooking is the *garam masala* ("hot spices"), a ground spice mixture made individually and uniquely by every cook. Here is The Grit's signature blend, used in our **Curry Dressing** and **Split Pea Dal**.

4 teaspoons curry powder
4 teaspoons cumin powder
3 teaspoons turmeric powder
3 teaspoons granulated garlic
3 teaspoons coriander powder
3 teaspoons cayenne pepper
2 teaspoons paprika
1 teaspoon dried ground ginger
1 teaspoon freshly ground cinnamon
1/3 teaspoon freshly ground nutmeg
1/3 teaspoon freshly ground clove

Combine well and store in an airtight container.

Yields 2/3 cup.

fundamentals

"The Grit is a great restaurant
and a source of local pride.
They have consummate taste."

—MICHAEL STIPE, R.E.M.

"Even if I was blessed with the culinary skills to create some of the dishes found on their menu, I would still frequent The Grit for the atmosphere. It serves as a port for my social life when I come home from tour or recording."

—BEN MIZE, COUNTING CROWS

"Whenever touring bands come to play at the 40 Watt Club and ask about a good place to eat I always send them to The Grit. Anyone who's been there once can't wait to mention that they're off to The Grit as soon as sound check is over."

—BARRIE BUCK, 40 WATT CLUB

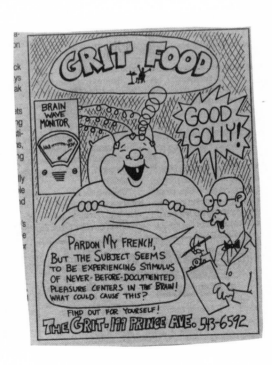

dressings

Customers have long appreciated The Grit's homemade salad dressings. Made from scratch with the right balance of acidity, sweetness, and saltiness, our regular dressings are rich and flavorful yet most are non-dairy, and our **Caesar Dressing** is a great vegetarian rendition. In a world of frighteningly gooey, guar gum- and carageenan-laden non-fat salad toppings, a restaurant that makes its own fresh dressings is bound to have devotees. And no dressing is more beloved than our vinaigrette, which figures in many other recipes in this book. Try them all and don't forget—it's all about emulsifying the oil and acid, so add that oil slowly for a smooth, pleasing result.

"The House Salad—I never thought I would ever crave a salad, I mean, it is just a salad, but I can't stop eating this thing!!! I dream about it! I think it has something to do with the magic they put in the lemon tahini dressing."

—DAN GELLER, I AM THE WORLD TRADE CENTER

- Grit Vinaigrette
- Creamy Garlic Dressing
- Feta Dressing
- Honey Mustard Dressing
- Lemon Tahini Dressing
- Curry Dressing
- Caesar Dressing
- Famous Vegan Ranch Dressing
- Roasted Garlic Vinaigrette

Dressings

Grit Vinaigrette

This dressing has such a pleasing, balanced, versatile flavor that beyond making a plain salad taste incredible, it is also a key ingredient in such Grit favorites as **Classic Grit Pasta Salad**, **Roma Tomato–Mozzarella Salad**, and **Chicken Salad-Style Tofu**. It also does wonders for practically any sandwich with lettuce or tomatoes.

    1/4 cup cider vinegar
    2 tablespoons red wine vinegar
    2 tablespoons balsamic vinegar
    6 tablespoons water
    4 tablespoons finely minced red onion
    2 small garlic cloves, chopped
    1 tablespoon sugar
    1/2 teaspoon salt
    1/2 teaspoon freshly ground black pepper
    Large pinch fresh or dried parsley
    Large pinch fresh or dried basil
    Large pinch fresh or dried oregano
    Large pinch fresh or dried thyme
    1 cup soybean oil

Combine all ingredients except oil in blender or food processor and mix well. Continue blending while adding oil in a slow, steady stream until smooth and thick. Use immediately or store tightly covered in the refrigerator for up to 2 weeks.

Yields 2 cups.

Creamy Garlic Dressing Ⓥ

Dressings

1/2 (15-ounce) block tofu, crumbled
6 tablespoons water
1/4 cup cider vinegar
3 small garlic cloves, chopped
3 tablespoons minced fresh parsley or 1 tablespoon dried
1-1/2 teaspoon dry mustard
1/2 teaspoon salt
1/8 teaspoon white pepper
3/4 cup soybean oil

Combine all ingredients except oil in blender or food processor and mix well. Continue blending while adding oil in a slow, steady stream until smooth and thick. Use immediately or store tightly covered in the refrigerator for up to 2 weeks.

Yields 2 cups.

Dressings

Feta Dressing

1 cup buttermilk
2/3 cup crumbled feta cheese
2 small garlic cloves, chopped
3 tablespoons cider vinegar
3/4 teaspoon freshly ground black
   pepper

1-1/2 teaspoon minced fresh dill or
   1/2 teaspoon dried
3/4 cup extra-virgin olive oil

Combine all ingredients except oil in blender or food processor and mix well. Continue blending while adding oil in a slow, steady stream until smooth and thick. Use immediately or store tightly covered in the refrigerator for up to 2 weeks.

Yields 2 cups.

Honey Mustard Dressing Ⓥ

Great over salad greens or as a zesty, sweet companion to our famous **Smelt** sandwich.

6 tablespoons Dijon mustard
1/4 cup cider vinegar
3 tablespoons honey
2 tablespoons water

2 small garlic cloves, chopped
1-1/2 teaspoons cumin powder
1/2 teaspoon white pepper
1 cup soybean oil

Combine all ingredients except oil in blender or food processor and mix well. Continue blending while adding oil in a slow, steady stream until smooth and thick. Use immediately or store tightly covered in the refrigerator for up to 2 weeks.

Yields 2 cups.

Lemon Tahini Dressing ⓥ

Dressings

1/2 (15-ounce) block tofu, crumbled
6 tablespoons freshly squeezed lemon juice
4 tablespoons tahini
1/2 cup water
2 small garlic cloves, chopped
1-1/2 teaspoon sugar
1-1/2 teaspoon cumin powder
1/2 teaspoon paprika
1/2 teaspoon salt
1/4 scant teaspoon cayenne pepper
1/2 cup soybean oil

Combine all ingredients except oil in blender or food processor and mix well.
Continue blending while adding oil in a slow, steady stream until smooth and thick.
Use immediately or store tightly covered in the refrigerator for up to 2 weeks.

Yields 2 cups.

"On tour, The Grit is like Mecca.
When I go to Athens I look forward
more to eating at The Grit than I do
to playing the gig."

—JULIANA HATFIELD

Dressings

1/2 (15-ounce) block tofu, crumbled
1/4 cup cider vinegar
1/4 cup water
3 tablespoons freshly squeezed lemon juice
1 tablespoon plus 1 teaspoon curry powder
1-1/2 teaspoons sugar
1/2 teaspoon salt
1 tablespoon Grit Indian Spice
3/4 cup soybean oil

Combine all ingredients except oil in blender or food processor and mix well. Continue blending while adding oil in a slow, steady stream until smooth and thick. Use immediately or store tightly covered in the refrigerator for up to 2 weeks.

Yields 2 cups.

If **Grit Indian Spice** is not available, increase curry powder by 1-1/2 teaspoons and add:

1/4 teaspoon granulated garlic
1/4 teaspoon dried ground ginger
1/4 teaspoon ground coriander
1/8 teaspoon cayenne pepper
1/8 teaspoon cumin powder
Pinch of freshly ground cinnamon

Caesar Dressing

1/2 (15-ounce) block tofu, crumbled
2 small garlic cloves, chopped
1/4 cup freshly squeezed lemon juice
2 tablespoons vegan Worcestershire sauce
1 tablespoon cider vinegar
1-1/2 teaspoon salt
1-1/2 teaspoon sugar
1 teaspoon freshly ground black pepper
1 cup extra-virgin olive oil
1 cup finely grated Parmesan cheese

Combine all ingredients except oil and cheese in blender or food processor and mix well. Continue blending while adding oil in a slow, steady stream until smooth and thick, then add cheese and continue to process until well combined. Use immediately or store tightly covered in the refrigerator for up to 2 weeks.

Yields 2 cups.

Dressings

Dressings

Famous Vegan Ranch Dressing Ⓥ

The flavor's really big 'n they'll never know it's vegan.

    1-1/2 cups vegan mayonnaise (Vegenaise brand is best)
    1/2 cup unsweetened soy milk
    1-1/2 teaspoons apple cider vinegar (we use Heinz)
    1-1/2 teaspoons nutritional yeast
    1-1/2 teaspoons onion powder
    1/4 teaspoon dried dill
    1/4 teaspoon black pepper
    1/4 teaspoon dry mustard
    1/4 teaspoon garlic powder

Combine all ingredients in a bowl and whisk until creamy and smooth. Use immediately or store tightly covered in the refrigerator for up to 2 weeks.

Yields 2 cups.

Dressings

Roasted Garlic Vinaigrette Dressing

1 whole bulb garlic
1 cup olive oil
1/2 cup balsamic vinegar
1/4 cup red wine vinegar
1/4 cup water
1 teaspoon salt
1 teaspoon sugar
1/2 teaspoon black pepper
1 large pinch dried basil
1 dash cayenne pepper

Preheat oven to 375°F.

Remove papery coating from garlic bulb carefully, without breaking cloves apart. Place in a small baking dish and drizzle with olive oil. Bake until garlic is soft and easily pierced with a thin knife (40 to 60 minutes). When done, peel and separate cloves. Extract all soft portions and combine with all other ingredients in a blender or food processor. Purée until smooth.

This recipe yields a thick dressing. If the result appears too thick, slowly and carefully add more water while blending until consistency is desirable. Use immediately or store tightly covered in the refrigerator for up to 2 weeks.

Yields 2 cups.

"I can hardly count the number of times The Grit has saved my life: perfect vittles in a wasteland of scary tour food."

—KRISTIN HERSH, THROWING MUSES

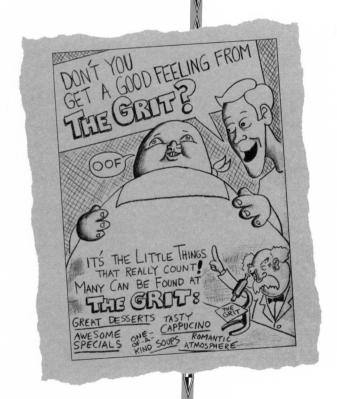

"The Grit has always been one of my favorite restaurants in Athens. I am so happy to now have a wonderful cookbook with all their great recipes."

—MARIANNE ROGERS,
Hee-Haw STAR

salads

When is a salad a meal? When it's a gargantuan heap of fresh greens and vegetables plentifully topped with succulent sautéed **Grit-Style Tofu** or shredded mild white Vermont cheddar and called **The Grit House Salad.** Or when you try one of these delicious cold salads made with sweet, zesty **Grit Vinaigrette Dressing** and decide that a side order won't do—you'd like an entire plateful, please. And if you love garlic, fresh lemon flavor, and great combos of herbs and spices, try the appetizers, too.

Salads

Tabouli V

While this classic grain dish is traditionally made with #1- or #2-size bulgur wheat, The Grit uses #3, a much larger grain. This makes for a distinctive version of tabouli, unusual but very enjoyable. Finely shredded ingredients in this recipe are best prepared with a shredding plate or blade in the food processor.

At The Grit we serve this salad on a bed of greens with our **Lemon Tahini Dressing**.

2 cups (#3) bulgur wheat
1/3 cup freshly squeezed lemon juice
2 tablespoons rice wine vinegar
2 cups boiling water
1/4 cup finely shredded seedless cucumber
1/4 cup finely shredded red radish
1/4 cup finely shredded carrot
1 large bunch fresh parsley, stems removed and finely minced

2 green onions (dark green parts only), finely minced
3/4 scant teaspoon salt
1/4 teaspoon freshly ground black pepper
1/4 teaspoon cumin powder
1/4 teaspoon granulated garlic

In a large bowl, combine bulgur wheat, lemon juice, and vinegar. Add boiling water until just covered and let sit until water is absorbed and bulgur is tender to the bite, approximately 30 to 45 minutes. Cool completely.

Add remaining ingredients and toss together until thoroughly mixed. Cover and refrigerate. Chill well. Serve alone or over salad greens.

Yields 6 servings.

"Whenever I'm in Athens, I try to have the Mid-E Platter with hummus, falafel, and tabouli at The Grit before I leave town. I feel incomplete and unfulfilled otherwise."

—DUANE DENISON, FORMERLY OF JESUS LIZARD

Green Bean Vinaigrette Salad with Fresh Mint ⓥ

Salads

12 cups water
1/2 teaspoon baking soda
1 pound green beans, tipped and
   trimmed
12 cups ice water
2/3 cup **Grit Vinaigrette**
2 tablespoons olive oil
1 tablespoon balsamic vinegar

1 generous teaspoon sugar
1 scant teaspoon salt
1/4 teaspoon freshly ground black
   pepper
Freshly squeezed juice of 1/2 lemon
Small fistful of fresh mint leaves
1 small or 1/2 large red onion,
   coarsely chopped

Combine water and baking soda in a large saucepan and bring to a boil. Drop beans in water, stir, and rapidly return the water to a boil. When beans are softened but still slightly firm to the bite and are a vibrant, dark green (4 to 5 minutes), remove from boiling water, drain, and quickly plunge into ice water; set aside.

   In food processor, combine all remaining ingredients except red onion. Process until well blended. Add red onion and pulse just until onion becomes very finely minced. Toss together all ingredients. Cover and refrigerate at least 2 hours. Serve well chilled.

Yields 5 servings.

Salads

Chickpea and Feta Salad

Simplicity made great, greatness made simple. Again with the help of our delicious **Grit Vinaigrette.**

> 2 (15.5-ounce) cans chickpeas (garbanzo beans), drained
> 1/2 medium red onion, finely minced
> 2 tablespoons minced fresh basil
> 2 cups finely crumbled feta cheese
> 1/2 cup **Grit Vinaigrette**
> 1/2 teaspoon salt
> 1/2 teaspoon freshly ground black pepper

Combine all ingredients and toss until well blended. Cover and refrigerate at least 1 hour. Serve well chilled alone or over salad greens.

Yields 4 servings.

Spicy Thai Noodles Ⓥ

Practically any sort of long, slender pasta will be fine for this recipe. If you can't find a 12-ounce package to use, measure as follows: grab a handful of 10-inch long noodles into a bundle slightly wider in diameter than a golf ball. There ya go!

12 ounces long, slender dried pasta, such as capellini, linguine, spaghetti, or vermicelli

4 quarts water

1 tablespoon salt

1/2 cup soy sauce

1/2 cup water

1/2 cup peanut butter

1/3 cup rice wine vinegar

1/4 cup sesame oil

1/4 cup honey

2 teaspoons chili paste or 1/2 teaspoon chili oil

2 teaspoons granulated garlic

1 teaspoon ginger powder

Freshly squeezed juice of 1 lime

5 green onions (dark green parts only), minced

1 cup snow peas or 1 cup frozen peas, thawed

1/2 cup slivered almonds

Combine water and salt in a large stockpot and bring to a boil. Add pasta to water and cook until al dente, about 8 minutes. Drain thoroughly in a large colander, rinse with cool water, and drain again; set aside.

Combine all other ingredients except green onions, peas, and almonds in a saucepan and stir well over high heat until gently boiling. Remove from heat. Toss noodles and sauce in a large bowl. Allow to cool slightly. Toss with remaining ingredients. Cover and refrigerate. Serve well chilled.

Yields 6 to 8 servings

Salads

Salads

Classic Grit Pasta Salad

The glorious return of the old-school combo of **Creamy Garlic** and **Vinaigrette Dressings**. Not only has it returned to the restaurant, but now it has come to your home.

12 cups water
1 tablespoon salt
4 cups dried medium shells, radiatore, or rotini
1 cup **Grit Vinaigrette**
1/2 cup **Creamy Garlic Dressing**
1 cup fresh cooked or frozen white corn
1/2 cup shredded carrots
1/2 cup freshly grated Parmesan cheese

3 green onions (dark green parts only), minced
3 tablespoons minced fresh parsley or 1 tablespoon dried
1/2 teaspoon salt
1/4 teaspoon freshly ground black pepper
2 tablespoons minced red bell pepper (optional)

Combine water and salt in a large stockpot and bring to a boil. Add pasta to water and cook until al dente, about 8 minutes. Drain thoroughly in a large colander, rinse with cool water, and drain again; set aside.

Combine pasta with remaining ingredients, toss together. Cover and refrigerate. Serve well chilled.

Yields 6 to 8 servings.

Roma Tomato—Mozzarella Salad

Salads

Use gorgeous tomatoes if you can . . . but even if your Romas aren't ravishing, this recipe will make them seem so!

- 1/2 medium red onion, cut into very thin crescents
- 1 small fistful of fresh basil leaves, finely minced
- 2/3 cup **Grit Vinaigrette**
- 2 tablespoons balsamic vinegar
- 1/4 cup extra-virgin olive oil
- 1/2 teaspoon sugar
- 1 teaspoon salt
- Large pinch of freshly ground black pepper
- 12 to 16 red Roma or plum tomatoes, sliced in half lengthwise, then cut into 3/8-inch thick "half-coins"
- 3 cups finely cubed (1/2-inch or less) mozzarella cheese (preferably fresh)

Combine all ingredients except tomatoes and mozzarella in a medium mixing bowl and stir well. Add tomatoes and mozzarella and gently toss together. Cover and refrigerate at least 1 hour. Serve well chilled.

Yields 6 to 8 servings.

Salads

Pecan Pesto Carrot Salad

This is one of those dishes that is greater than the sum of its parts. Such gigantic flavor from so few ingredients! But look closely—one of them is **Grit Vinaigrette**. That explains it!

1 small fistful of fresh basil leaves
1/2 cup chopped pecans
3 tablespoons freshly grated
   Parmesan cheese
1-1/2 teaspoon sugar
Extra-virgin olive oil

5 cups finely shredded carrots
1/4 cup **Grit Vinaigrette**
2 teaspoons freshly squeezed lemon
   juice
1 teaspoon salt

Combine basil, pecans, cheese, and sugar in a food processor. Slowly add enough olive oil to make a pesto and blend until smooth.

Combine pesto with remaining ingredients, stir together well. Cover and refrigerate. Serve well chilled alone or over salad greens.

Yields 6 servings.

"The top of my list of things to do in Athens is hit The Grit."
—TRAVIS MCNABB,
BETTER THAN EZRA

Tropical Corn Salad

A bright, spicy, and refreshing concoction with jalapeño and fresh fruit flavor.

1 cup very finely minced red onion
Finely minced leaves of 7 to 10
   cilantro stems
1 small or 1/2 large jalapeño chile,
   very finely minced
1/2 to 2/3 cup finely chopped fresh
   pineapple
1/3 cup freshly squeezed lime juice
2 tablespoons cider vinegar

2 teaspoons hot sauce
1-1/2 teaspoon salt
1 teaspoon sugar
1/4 teaspoon freshly ground black
   pepper
6 cups fresh cooked or frozen white
   corn, thawed
Butter or margarine

Combine all ingredients except corn and butter or margarine in a large mixing bowl. Mix well. Cover and refrigerate.

Lightly sauté corn in minimal amount of butter or margarine. Cool corn thoroughly. Toss corn with refrigerated mixture. Cover and refrigerate at least 1 hour. Serve well chilled.

Yields 5 servings.

Salads

eat grit...
KEEP FIT
THE GRIT
199 PRINCE AVE. • 543-6592
MON-FRI 11AM-10PM
SAT-SUN 10AM-3PM / 5PM-10PM
8/23/95

"Whenever I visit my old stomping grounds of Athens, Georgia, my first stop is always The Grit! The food and the company at The Grit rule—and that's a fact. Save me a seat."

—KATE PIERSON, THE B-52'S

"Everybody I know that's on tour or from out of town wants to go straight to The Grit. It's world renowned!"

—BILL DOSS,
OLIVIA TREMOR CONTROL

soups

Soups should be simple. Yet soup at The Grit can confuse people. "This cream soup is so rich it must have dairy in it," diners will say to the wait staff. "But the menu doesn't say so. Will you go ask the cook if it's vegan?"

"Yup, it's vegan!" will be the answer.

Or a customer will ask, "What about that great soup I had here a while back? It was Roasted Garlic-Something. When will you have it again?"

"Sorry, there was a bunch of extra roasted garlic that day and that soup just got thrown together!" they'll be told.

So . . . let's nail some stuff down! Following are 19 handy soup recipes, ranging from curried **Split Pea Dal**, available every day in our restaurant, to **Irish Mock-Beef Stew**, which we make only on St. Patrick's Day. Although hearty, most are vegan. All are satisfying and soothing, as soup should be.

Chilled Soups

Gazpacho Ⓥ

The canned tomato items used here can be refrigerated prior to opening so you can sooner enjoy the thrill of the chill.

I small or 1/2 large red onion, finely minced

2 large ripe tomatoes, seeded and finely chopped (enough to yield 2 cups)

I scant teaspoon minced fresh garlic

1/2 medium green bell pepper, seeded and coarsely chopped

1/4 medium jalapeño chile, finely chopped

2 cups spring or filtered water

I (46-ounce) can vegetable-juice cocktail, such as V-8 juice

I (28-ounce) can diced tomatoes

I small or 1/2 large seedless cucumber, finely shredded

Freshly squeezed juice of 2 lemons

3 tablespoons cider vinegar

I tablespoon red wine vinegar

I tablespoon extra-virgin olive oil

I teaspoon hot sauce, or more to taste

2 tablespoons chopped fresh basil or 2 teaspoons dried

2 tablespoons chopped fresh parsley or 2 teaspoons dried

2-1/2 teaspoons salt

1/2 teaspoon freshly ground black pepper

1/4 teaspoon cumin powder

Place 1/2 of prepared onion, 1/2 of prepared fresh tomato, garlic, green pepper, and chile in a food processor and puree until liquified, adding water if necessary. Thoroughly combine all ingredients in a large, non-metal bowl. Cover tightly and refrigerate at least 4 hours. Serve very cold in chilled bowls.

Yields 12 to 14 servings.

Chilled Tomato and Avocado Soup

4 ripe medium avocados
2 (15-ounce) cans diced tomatoes
1 (11.5-ounce) can vegetable-juice
  cocktail, such as V-8 juice
1 cup spring or filtered water
1 ripe medium tomato, seeded and
  chopped
1 small red onion, finely chopped
1/2 teaspoon minced fresh garlic

1 small jalapeño chile, finely chopped
1 bunch fresh cilantro, stems
  removed
Freshly squeezed juice of 1 lemon
2-1/4 teaspoon salt
1/2 teaspoon freshly ground black
  pepper

Peel and pit avocados. Cut 1 avocado into small cubes and set aside. Slice remaining avocados. Reserve 1 can of diced tomatoes and set aside.

Puree 3 sliced avocados with remaining ingredients in a food processor. When smoothly blended, pour into a large, non-metal bowl. Stir in avocado cubes and reserved can of diced tomatoes. Cover tightly and refrigerate at least 4 hours. Serve very cold in chilled bowls.

Yields 10 to 12 servings.

Chilled Soups

Tomato Garlic Soup Ⓥ

A simple soup with a satisfying tang and a lot of great garlic flavor.

2 whole bulbs or approximately
   1/3 cup garlic cloves, peeled
2 large yellow onions, finely chopped
Extra-virgin olive oil
3 large ripe tomatoes, seeded and
   finely chopped (enough to yield
   3 cups)
1/3 cup cider vinegar
1/4 cup vegan Worcestershire sauce

1 heaping tablespoon salt
1 generous teaspoon Dijon mustard
1 teaspoon granulated garlic
3/4 teaspoon freshly ground black
   pepper
2 (28-ounce) cans diced tomatoes
5 cups water
1 heaping teaspoon cornstarch

In food processor, grind garlic cloves and 1/2 of chopped onion until pureed. Add remaining chopped onion and grind on pulse setting, just until second addition of onion is very finely minced. Put in a small bowl; set aside.

Cover bottom of a large stockpot with a thin layer of olive oil and place over high heat. Add garlic and onion mixture and stir well, cooking until deeply browned. As onion and garlic cook, puree fresh tomatoes in food processor. Add to browned onion and garlic and cook over high heat, stirring often. Add remaining ingredients except canned tomatoes, water, and cornstarch. Simmer mixture vigorously for at least 5 minutes.

Puree canned tomatoes in food processor and add to soup with spring water. In a small bowl, blend cornstarch with enough hot soup to make a thin paste free of lumps. Add paste to soup. Simmer gently for 5 minutes until thick. Serve hot in warmed bowls.

Yields 10 to 12 servings.

Tomato, Basil, and Feta Soup

3-1/2 cups water
1/3 cup soy sauce
1 teaspoon onion powder
2 tablespoons extra-virgin olive oil
1 small onion, finely chopped
2 teaspoons minced garlic
1 small red bell pepper, finely chopped
1 teaspoon salt

1/2 teaspoon freshly ground black pepper
2 (15-ounce) cans diced tomatoes
1/2 cup finely chopped fresh basil
1 teaspoon balsamic vinegar
2 teaspoons cornstarch
Water
Freshly squeezed juice of 1 lemon
1 cup finely crumbled feta cheese

Thoroughly combine water, soy sauce, and onion powder in a small mixing bowl; set aside.

Heat olive oil in a large stockpot and add onion. Sauté until softened and add garlic and red bell pepper. Sauté 3 to 4 minutes. Add salt, pepper, diced tomatoes, and soy sauce mixture. Stirring often, bring to a boil. Reduce heat and add basil and vinegar. Blend cornstarch into just enough water to dissolve without lumps and stir into soup. Simmer for 15 to 20 minutes and remove from heat. Stir in lemon juice and crumbled feta cheese. Serve hot in warmed bowls.

Yields 5 to 7 servings.

"Where else in the world can you get soup served by the singer/songwriter of Jucifer? Life is beautiful."

—KEVN KINNEY, DRIVIN' N' CRYIN'

Hearty Soups

Roasted Red Pepper and Mushroom Soup Ⓥ

1 (12-ounce) jar roasted red peppers
3-1/2 cups water
1/3 cup soy sauce
1 teaspoon onion powder
2 tablespoons vegan margarine
1 small yellow onion, finely chopped
1 teaspoon minced garlic
3 cups trimmed and sliced button or
  cremini mushrooms
1/2 cup all-purpose flour
1 teaspoon salt
1/2 teaspoon freshly ground black
  pepper

1/2 teaspoon dry mustard
1 tablespoon chopped fresh parsley
  or 1 teaspoon dried
2-1/4 teaspoons chopped fresh
  rosemary or 1/4 teaspoon dried
2-2/4 teaspoons chopped fresh
  thyme or 1/4 teaspoon dried
1 tablespoon plus 1 teaspoon vegan
  Worcestershire sauce
2 cups soy milk

Puree roasted red peppers with their liquid in a food processor; set aside. Thoroughly combine water, soy sauce, and onion powder in a small bowl; set aside.

Melt margarine in a large stockpot and add onion and garlic. Sauté until onions are translucent. Add mushrooms and sauté until tender. Add flour, salt, pepper, dried mustard, herbs, and Worcestershire sauce. Cook over gentle heat, stirring frequently, for 5 minutes. Increase heat and gradually stir in soy sauce mixture, then pureed red peppers, then soy milk. Simmer, stirring frequently, for 15 minutes. Serve hot in warmed bowls.

Yields 6 to 8 servings.

Onion Dijon Soup

One of our most highly complimented soups, given here in a large batch.

1 (14.5-ounce) can cut green beans, drained, with liquid reserved

1/4 cup plus 1 teaspoon extra-virgin olive oil

1/4 cup soy sauce

3 medium garlic cloves, minced

5 large yellow onions, sliced into fine, delicate crescents (enough to yield 10 cups)

1 cup apple juice

1/2 cup white wine

1/2 cup vegan Worcestershire sauce

1/4 cup cider vinegar

1 tablespoon plus 1 teaspoon Dijon mustard

1-1/2 teaspoon salt

1/4 teaspoon freshly ground black pepper

1-3/4 cups vegetable stock or water

Pour 1 teaspoon olive oil in a large, heavy skillet and place over high heat. Add green beans, soy sauce, and garlic. Sauté until beans are tender and liquid has thickened and intensified. Place contents of skillet in food processor and puree; set aside.

In a large stockpot, heat 1/4 cup olive oil over high heat. Add onions and sauté until translucent. Add remaining ingredients except water or vegetable stock and reserved green bean liquid. Simmer covered, stirring often, until onions are extremely tender. Add stock or water and green bean liquid. Bring to a gentle boil and simmer for 15 minutes. Serve hot in warmed bowls.

Yields 12 to 14 servings.

Hearty Soups

Vegetable Stock

Vegetable stock can be made from a catch-all of ingredients— a little of this and a little of that. The recipe below is a guideline but use what you have on hand—even vegetables that might be a little past their prime—and adjust and season to your taste. The secret is to start with cold water and to never boil the mixture. This stock can be made 4 days ahead and it keeps frozen 3 months.

   Many of our soup recipes call for a mixture of soy sauce, water, and onion powder—our version of an instant stock—but a slow-cooked vegetable stock could always be used in its place.

3 medium yellow onions, chopped

3 tablespoons vegan margarine or butter

2 large carrots, coarsely chopped

2 celery ribs, coarsely chopped

2 leeks (white and pale green parts only), washed well, trimmed, and chopped

Peels of 2 large potatoes (enough to yield 1 cup)

cont'd ➤

Split Pea Dal ⓥ

1 pound dried green split peas, rinsed
2 quarts water
1 small or 1/2 large yellow onion, finely chopped
2 teaspoons minced fresh garlic
1-1/2 teaspoon salt
1-1/2 teaspoon curry powder
1-1/2 teaspoon Grit Indian Spice

Combine all ingredients in a large stockpot. Bring to a boil, stirring frequently. Reduce heat and simmer for 1 hour, stirring very frequently. When consistency is creamy and split peas have lost their body, soup is done.

   For a delightful creamier result, puree cooked soup in a blender or food processor. Reheat and serve immediately in warmed bowls.

Yields 6 to 8 servings.

If you don't have Grit Indian Spice on hand, increase curry powder by 1/2 teaspoon and add:

    1/4 teaspoon granulated garlic
    1/4 teaspoon ginger powder
    1/4 teaspoon dried coriander
    1/8 teaspoon cayenne pepper
    1/8 teaspoon cumin powder

"For some reason, Thursday is split pea soup day in most American eateries. Well, I have to tell you what a treat it was that The Grit serves split pea soup every day of the week and, even better, it's curried pea soup. What a unique idea! What a surprising taste treat."

—SPALDING GRAY

Spinach and Lentil Soup

Another great use for **Grit Marinara**. If you are without, we've provided a substitute. But you know it won't be quite the same, don't you?

- 1 (10-ounce) package frozen chopped spinach, thawed and drained
- 3-1/2 quarts (14 cups) water
- 1-1/2 cups brown lentils, picked over and rinsed
- 1 small or 1/2 large yellow onion, finely chopped
- 2 medium carrots, peeled and cut in 1/4-inch-thick coins
- 2 stalks celery, finely chopped
- 2 teaspoons minced garlic
- 1/4 cup plus 1 tablespoon cider vinegar

- 2 tablespoons soy sauce
- 2 teaspoons salt
- 1 generous teaspoon Dijon mustard
- 1/4 teaspoon freshly ground black pepper
- 1/8 scant teaspoon or 1 large pinch of white pepper
- 2-1/2 cups **Grit Marinara** or 1 (28-ounce) can crushed tomatoes, salt, and Italian spices (dried or fresh parsley, oregano, and basil) to taste

Combine all ingredients except **Grit Marinara** or tomato mixture and spinach in a large stockpot and bring to a boil, stirring frequently. Cook until lentils begin to soften, 20 to 30 minutes. Add **Grit Marinara** or tomato mixture and cook until lentils and carrots are fully tender, 10 to 15 minutes. Add spinach and cook for 1 or 2 minutes. Serve immediately in warmed bowls.

Yields 12 to 14 servings.

- 1/4 pound button or cremini mushrooms, chopped
- 12-1/3 cups cold water (divided)
- 6 garlic cloves, unpeeled
- 1/2 teaspoon dried thyme
- 2 bay leaves
- 12 sprigs of fresh parsley
- 1 teaspoon salt
- 1/2 teaspoon black peppercorns

In a large stockpot over moderate heat, sauté onions in butter or margarine until golden. Add carrots, celery, leeks, potato peelings, mushrooms, and enough water to cover and simmer, covered, stirring occasionally, for 5 minutes. Add remaining 12 cups water, garlic, thyme, bay leaves, parsley, peppercorns, and salt and return to a simmer. Simmer mixture, uncovered, until vegetables have yielded all of their flavor and are completely soft, about 2 hours. Strain stock through a fine sieve into a heatproof bowl and cool, uncovered. Skim fat before using.

Yields approximately 9 cups.

Hearty Soups

Thai Coconut Soup V

A tangy new lovin' ladle-full from The Grit.

2 cups water
1 (14-ounce) can coconut milk
1 vegetable bouillon cube
Freshly squeezed juice of 2 limes
3 tablespoons freshly squeezed
  lemon juice
2 tablespoons soy sauce
1 tablespoon chili oil

1 tablespoon ginger powder
2 teaspoons brown sugar
1/2 teaspoon chili paste
1 block firm tofu, cut into small
  cubes
3 cups sliced mushrooms
2 tablespoons minced fresh cilantro

Combine water and coconut milk in a 2-quart saucepan over high heat. When it boils, dissolve bouillon cube into the mixture. Reduce heat to a simmer and stir in citrus juices, soy sauce, chili oil and paste, ginger powder, and brown sugar. Add tofu, mushrooms, and cilantro and simmer for 20 minutes, stirring occasionally.

Serve immediately in warmed bowls.

Yields 4 to 6 servings.

Cream of Onion Soup V

4 tablespoons vegan margarine
3 large yellow onions, thinly sliced
1 tablespoon plus 1 teaspoon onion
  powder
1 teaspoon salt
1 scant teaspoon white pepper
1 teaspoon rubbed sage or
  1/2 teaspoon ground sage
1 tablespoon chopped fresh parsley
  or 1 teaspoon dried

1-1/2 teaspoon fresh chopped thyme
  or 1/2 teaspoon dried
1/2 cup all-purpose flour
1/4 cup nutritional yeast
5 cups water
1/2 cup soy sauce
3 tablespoons vegan Worcestershire
  sauce
1-1/2 cups soy milk

Melt margarine in a large stockpot and add onions. Sauté until onions are tender and translucent. Stir in onion powder, salt, pepper, and herbs and sauté 2 minutes. Add flour and yeast. Cook over gentle heat, stirring frequently, for 5 minutes.

Increase heat and gradually stir in soy sauce mixture, then Worcestershire sauce. Simmer for 15 to 20 minutes. Add soy milk and return to simmer. Serve immediately in warmed bowls.

Yields 6 to 8 servings.

Creamy Soups

- **Cream of Onion Soup**
- **Cream of Tomato Soup**
- **Mock Cream of Chicken Soup**
- **Jimmy Ray's Butternut Poblano Soup**
- **Cream of Asparagus Soup**

Creamy Soups

Cream of Tomato Soup V

This soup is pureed to achieve its creamy consistency.

3-1/2 cups water
1/3 cup soy sauce
1 teaspoon onion powder
2 tablespoons vegan margarine
1 small yellow onion, finely chopped
2 stalks celery, finely chopped
1 teaspoon minced garlic
1/2 cup all-purpose flour
2 teaspoons salt
1/2 teaspoon freshly ground black
  pepper

1/2 teaspoon dry mustard
Very small pinch of freshly ground
  nutmeg
1 (28-ounce) can crushed tomatoes,
  undrained
1 (15-ounce) can diced tomatoes,
  undrained
1-1/2 cups soy milk

Combine water, soy sauce, and onion powder; set aside.

Melt margarine in large stockpot and add onion, celery, and garlic. Sauté over medium-high heat until onions are translucent, celery is tender, and garlic is soft, approximately 5 minutes. Add flour, salt, pepper, dry mustard, and nutmeg. Stirring frequently, cook over gentle heat for 5 minutes. Increase heat and gradually add soy sauce mixture, stirring vigorously until mixture is smooth. Add crushed and diced tomatoes, stir well, and simmer for 20 minutes.

Stir in soy milk. When soup returns to a simmer, puree in a blender or food processor. Reheat and serve immediately in warmed bowls.

Yields 8 to 10 servings.

Mock Cream of Chicken Soup Ⓥ

Creamy Soups

This soup features chicken-flavored T.V.P. (textured vegetable protein), an unglamorous name for a great product that can often make the difference between a vegetarian dish that satisfies and one that doesn't. Also called for is vegetarian "chicken stock" powder. Both ingredients are available at most natural food stores.

3/4 cup dried T.V.P. in small, light
  chunks
Boiling water to cover T.V.P.
2 tablespoons "chicken stock"
  powder
6 cups hot water
2 tablespoons vegan margarine
1 small yellow onion, finely minced
2 stalks celery, finely chopped
1/2 cup all-purpose flour
1/2 cup nutritional yeast
1-1/2 teaspoon salt
1/2 teaspoon white pepper

1/2 teaspoon onion powder
1 tablespoon chopped fresh parsley
  or 1 teaspoon dried
1/2 teaspoon rubbed sage or 1/4
  teaspoon ground sage
1-1/2 cups soy milk
1/4 cup white wine
1 tablespoon Dijon mustard
1 tablespoon hot sauce
1 tablespoon vegan Worcestershire
  sauce
1 tablespoon soy sauce

Soak T.V.P. in enough hot water to cover; set aside. Stir "chicken stock" powder into 1-1/2 quarts hot water; set aside.

Melt margarine in a large stockpot and add onion and celery. Sauté until onions are translucent and celery is tender, about 5 minutes. Add flour, yeast, salt, pepper, onion powder, and herbs. Stirring frequently, cook over gentle heat for 5 minutes. Increase heat and gradually add soy milk, stirring vigorously until mixture is smooth. Add prepared T.V.P., prepared "chicken stock" mixture, and remaining ingredients. Simmer gently, stirring frequently, for 20 minutes. Serve immediately in warmed bowls.

Yields 6 to 8 servings.

For a richer version of this soup, substitute butter for vegan margarine and whole dairy milk for soy milk.

Creamy Soups

Jimmy Ray's Butternut Poblano Soup Ⓥ

Oven-roasted squash and peppers make a magic medley of sweet, spicy, and creamy flavors.

1 large butternut squash	1 tablespoon salt
1 large or 2 small poblano peppers	1 tablespoon chili powder
3 cups soy milk	1 tablespoon dried parsley
1/2 cup (1 stick) vegan margarine	1 teaspoon black pepper
1 large yellow onion, diced	1 teaspoon coriander
1 stalk celery, finely chopped	1/4 teaspoon cinnamon
3 tablespoons minced garlic	1 dash dried rosemary
2 tablespoons white flour	2 cups vegetable stock or water

Preheat oven to 400°F. Cut the butternut squash in half lengthwise and remove the seeds and pulp with a spoon. Place the squash skin side up on a baking sheet with just enough water in the pan to cover its bottom. Roast for 45 minutes or until the squash is soft to the touch and easily pierced by a utensil. Set aside to cool.

Roast whole poblano pepper(s) at 400°F for 15 minutes, turning halfway through roasting time, and remove from heat when the skin is blistered and flesh softened. Allow peppers to cool. Pull gently on the stem to remove it and the seed pod within (discard both). Chop the remaining pepper very finely.

Use a spoon to scoop the flesh from the squash. Place squash in a blender or food processor with soy milk. Purée until very smooth. Set aside.

In a large stockpot, melt margarine over medium heat and add onion, celery, and garlic. Sauté for approximately 15 minutes, stirring often, until onions and celery are soft. Stir in flour, salt, and remaining dry spices to form a paste. Stirring almost constantly, cook the paste over just enough heat to maintain a slight but steady bubbling for approximately 6 minutes. Slowly stir in the vegetable stock or water, and the prepared poblano pepper. Simmer for 5 minutes, stirring often. Slowly add the squash and soy milk mixture, stirring often, and cook for 10 minutes.

Serve immediately in warmed bowls.

Yields 6 servings.

Cream of Asparagus Soup

Choose from the very rich traditional style or delicious dairy-free version of this beloved soup.

2 tablespoons white flour
2 tablespoons minced fresh parsley
   or 1 tablespoon dried parsley
1 tablespoon nutritional yeast
1 tablespoon salt
1 teaspoon black pepper
1 teaspoon dry mustard
1/2 teaspoon dried marjoram
1/2 teaspoon oregano
1/4 teaspoon white pepper
1/4 teaspoon dried dill
1 dash cayenne pepper
2 cups water or vegetable stock

1/4 cup white wine
4 cups frozen cut asparagus or
   5 cups fresh asparagus (with hard
   portions removed from base of
   stem) chopped in 1-inch lengths
1/2 cup (1 stick) butter or vegan
   margarine for dairy-free version
1 large yellow onion, diced
1 stalk celery, finely chopped
1 tablespoon plus 1 teaspoon minced
   garlic
3 cups whole milk or unsweetened
   soy milk for dairy-free version

Combine the 11 dry ingredients and set aside.

Place water or vegetable stock and white wine in a saucepan over high heat. Add asparagus and, if necessary, a small amount of water to cover asparagus. Boil until asparagus is dark green and very tender. Set aside asparagus in water or stock.

In a 4-quart stockpot, melt butter or margarine over medium heat. Add onions, celery, and garlic and sauté until onions are translucent and celery is soft. Add dry ingredient mixture, and stir thoroughly to form a thick paste. Cook over enough heat to maintain a steady bubbling, stirring almost constantly, for approximately 5 minutes. Slowly add milk or soy milk and stir well. Cook over medium heat for 10 minutes, stirring frequently. Add asparagus and stock and cook for 5 minutes.

Transfer to a blender or food processor and purée until smooth and creamy. Return soup to stockpot and simmer for 5 minutes. Serve immediately in warmed bowls.

Yields 6 servings.

Creamy Soups

Scotch Broth

The Grit's incredibly hearty "beef stew" happens to be vegan—yet loved by all who try it. Chunky beef-style T.V.P. (textured vegetable protein), available at many natural food stores, makes it all happen.

1 large boiling or Yukon Gold potato, peeled and cut into 1/2-inch cubes
3-1/2 cups water
1/3 cup soy sauce
1 teaspoon onion powder
1 cup chunky beef-style T.V.P.
Boiling water to cover T.V.P.
2 tablespoons vegan margarine
1 small yellow onion, finely chopped
1 medium carrot, peeled and thinly sliced
1 leek (white and pale green parts only), finely chopped
1/4 cup all-purpose flour
1/4 cup nutritional yeast
1 teaspoon salt
1/2 teaspoon freshly ground black pepper
1 teaspoon dry mustard
1/2 teaspoon rubbed sage or 1/4 teaspoon ground sage
1/4 cup tomato puree
1/2 cup Guinness Stout or other stout beer (optional)
1/2 cup peas, fresh or frozen

Boil potatoes in a mixture of water, soy sauce, and onion powder until barely tender; set aside.

Melt margarine in large stockpot and add onion, carrot, and leek. Sauté, stirring often, until vegetables are tender, about 10 minutes. Add flour, yeast, salt, pepper, mustard, and sage. Cook over gentle heat, stirring often, for 10 minutes. Gradually stir in boiled potato mixture and increase heat until simmering. Add T.V.P., tomato puree, and beer. Simmer, stirring often, for 15 to 20 minutes. Serve immediately in warmed bowls.

Yields 6 to 8 servings.

Winter Vegetable Stew Ⓥ

With the magical flavor of parsnips.

1 medium parsnip, peeled and cut into 1/4-inch cubes

1 medium boiling or Yukon Gold potato, peeled and cut into 1/2-inch cubes

5 cups water

1/2 cup soy milk

1 tablespoon onion powder

1/4 cup Guinness Stout or other stout beer

2 tablespoons vegan Worcestershire sauce

4 tablespoons vegan margarine

1 small yellow onion, finely chopped

1 carrot, peeled and thinly chopped

2 stalks celery, finely chopped

1 medium leek (white and pale green parts only), thinly sliced

1/2 cup all-purpose flour

1/4 cup nutritional yeast

1 teaspoon salt

1/2 teaspoon freshly ground black pepper

1/2 teaspoon dry mustard

Very small pinch of nutmeg

1 bay leaf

Pinch of fresh or dried sage

Pinch of fresh or dried rosemary

Pinch of fresh or dried thyme

1/2 cup corn, fresh or frozen

1 cup soy milk

Boil parsnip and potato in a blend of water, soy sauce, onion powder, beer, and Worcestershire sauce until barely tender; set aside.

Melt margarine in a large stockpot and add onion, carrot, celery, and leek. Sauté until vegetables are tender. Add flour, yeast, salt, black pepper, dry mustard, nutmeg, and herbs, and cook over gentle heat for 5 minutes. Increase heat and gradually stir in boiled parsnip and potato mixture. Simmer, stirring frequently, for 15 to 20 minutes. Add corn and soy milk and simmer for 5 minutes. Remove and discard bay leaf. Serve immediately in warmed bowls.

Yields 6 to 8 servings.

A Few Stews and One Wonderful Chowder

A Few Stews and One Wonderful Chowder

"Beef"-and-Barley Vegetable Stew Ⓥ

1/2 cup chunky beef-style T.V.P. (textured vegetable protein)
Boiling water to cover T.V.P.
3-1/2 cups water
1/3 cup soy sauce
1 teaspoon onion powder
2 tablespoons extra-virgin olive oil
1 small yellow onion, finely chopped
1 medium carrot, peeled and thinly sliced
2 stalks celery, finely chopped
1 small boiling or Yukon Gold potato, peeled and cut into 1/2-inch cubes
1 cup trimmed and sliced button or cremini mushrooms
1/2 cup peas, fresh or frozen
1 small zucchini, finely chopped
1/4 cup medium pearl barley
Water
2 tablespoons all-purpose flour
1/2 cup nutritional yeast
1 teaspoon salt
1/2 teaspoon freshly ground black pepper
1/2 teaspoon dry mustard
2-1/2 teaspoons chopped fresh thyme or 1/4 teaspoon dried
1/4 teaspoon rubbed sage or pinch of ground sage
1 (15-ounce) can diced tomatoes

Cover T.V.P. with boiling water; set aside. Combine water, soy sauce, and onion powder; set aside.

Heat olive oil in a large stockpot and add onion, carrot, celery, and potato. Sauté until vegetables are barely tender. Add mushrooms, peas, zucchini, barley, and a small amount of water. Sauté until vegetables are fully tender, stirring frequently. Add flour, yeast, salt, pepper, dry mustard, and herbs. Cook over gentle heat for 5 minutes. Increase heat and gradually stir in soy sauce mixture, then tomatoes and T.V.P. Simmer 15 to 20 minutes, stirring frequently. Serve immediately in warmed bowls.

Yields 6 to 8 servings.

Irish Mock Beef Stew

Yes, we serve it on St. Patrick's Day with our **Irish Soda Bread.** People freak over it, so we probably should break it out more often!

2 cups chunky beef-style T.V.P. (textured vegetable protein)

3-1/2 cups water

2 medium boiling or Yukon Gold potatoes, peeled and cut in 1-inch cubes

1 small or 1/2 large yellow onion, finely chopped

2 cups carrots, peeled and sliced 3/8-inch thick

2 stalks celery, finely chopped

2 quarts boiling water

1/2 cup butter

1/2 cup all-purpose flour

5 tablespoons nutritional yeast

3/4 cup whole milk

1/4 cup soy sauce

3 tablespoons vegan Worcestershire sauce

3 tablespoons Guinness Stout or other stout beer

2-1/2 teaspoons salt

3/4 teaspoon freshly ground black pepper

1/4 teaspoon rubbed sage or pinch of ground sage

Combine T.V.P. and 3-1/2 cups water in a saucepan and bring to a boil; remove from heat and set aside.

In a large stockpot, vigorously boil potatoes, onion, carrots, and celery in 2 quarts water just until vegetables are tender, approximately 10 minutes.

In a saucepan over low heat, heat butter just until melted. Stir in flour and yeast and whisk vigorously over just enough heat to make mixture bubble. Cook 4 minutes to form a roux. Add milk and soy sauce in 3 or 4 portions, stirring thoroughly after each addition and allowing mixture to thicken between additions (this may require increased heat). When fully combined and thickened, remove from heat.

Gently stir roux into vegetable mixture and bring to a gentle boil. Add remaining ingredients. Reduce to a simmer for 5 minutes or until vegetables are extremely tender but retain their body. Serve immediately in warmed bowls.

Yields 8 to 10 servings.

Drink remaining Guinness from open bottle and act lewdly until police arrive. Remove clothing and go into fetal position (it's been a long day in the kitchen).

A Few Stews and One Wonderful Chowder

A Few Stews and One Wonderful Chowder

Corn and Potato Chowder Ⓥ

2 medium boiling or Yukon Gold
   potatoes, peeled and cut into
   1/2-inch cubes
3-1/2 cups water
1/3 cup soy sauce
1 teaspoon onion powder
2 tablespoons vegan margarine
1 small yellow onion, finely chopped
1 medium carrot, peeled and thinly
   sliced
2 stalks celery, finely chopped

1/2 cup all-purpose flour
1 teaspoon salt
1/2 teaspoon freshly ground black
   pepper
1-1/2 teaspoon chopped fresh
   parsley or 1/2 teaspoon dried
Pinch of fresh or dried thyme
Pinch of fresh or dried oregano
2 cups soy milk
1-1/2 cup corn, fresh or frozen

Boil potatoes in a mixture of water, soy sauce, and onion powder until barely tender; set aside.

Melt margarine in a large stockpot and add onion, carrot, and celery. Sauté over medium heat until vegetables are tender, approximately 5 minutes. Add flour, salt, pepper, and herbs. Cook over gentle heat, stirring often, for 10 minutes. Increase heat and gradually stir in potato mixture, then soy milk and corn. Simmer for 15 to 20 minutes, stirring frequently. Serve immediately in warmed bowls.

Yields 6 to 8 servings.

breads

When people talk about the "loafers" working at The Grit, we can only assume they are referring to the busy bread-makers back in the kitchen, stretching and forming dough by hand for each six-loaf mini-batch of **Ted Bread**. This longtime favorite is nothing fancy, yet it's hearty and versatile (it's great for sandwiches and also makes a mean French toast). Our popular **Grit Cornbread** is also baked daily, and recipes for these two regulars are joined here by a few other Grit originals.

"I consider it a true southern show of benevolence and generosity that the Grit put their cornbread recipe into print. I lived in Athens for 6 years before I stumbled upon the Grit's cornbread. I didn't even know it was on the menu. I think most people don't know of it or else they'd consume it by the plateful like I do. It's a meal all on its own, the BEST I have ever eaten, and please don't tell my mama or grandma I said so."

—CLAIRE CAMPBELL, HOPE FOR A GOLDEN SUMMER

Breads

Ted Bread

This very fast-rising bread is made for toasting. Use it for a grilled cheese, a.k.a. **The Smelt**, or to make dynamite French toast.

  1-1/2 cups very warm (105°F max) water
  1 tablespoon fast-rising dry yeast
  1 tablespoon plus 1 teaspoon sugar
  1-1/2 teaspoons salt
  1/4 cup soybean oil
  2-3/4 cups all-purpose flour
  1-1/2 cups whole wheat flour

In mixing bowl, combine water, yeast, sugar, and salt. Stir and allow to sit 5 to 10 minutes. Blend in oil, then flours. Stir together well and knead for at least 3 minutes in bread mixer or by hand on floured surface. Place in bowl covered loosely with plastic wrap and allow to rise in warm place (75° to 80°F) until nearly doubled in size, approximately 40 minutes.

Preheat oven to 375°F. Grease an 8-1/2 x 4-1/2-inch (6 cup) loaf pan.

Punch down dough and form into a rounded loaf shape, gently tuck dough towards center of bottom, slightly stretching top to a smooth tightness. Place in prepared pan and allow to rise for 5 minutes in warm place (75° to 80°F). Bake on the middle oven rack for approximately 35 minutes until nicely browned and hollow-sounding when tapped on bottom. Cool for 10 minutes in pan, then remove bread to a wire rack to cool completely.

Yields 1 loaf or 10 servings.

Freezes well for later use.

Old-Time Grit Buns Ⓥ

Breads

Please use regular soy milk, not reduced or non-fat.

- 1-1/3 cup plus 1 tablespoon very warm (about 105°F) soy milk
- 2 tablespoons sugar
- 1 tablespoon fast-rising dry yeast
- 1-1/4 teaspoon salt
- 1/2 cup vegetable oil
- 2-3/4 cups all-purpose flour
- 1/4 cup whole wheat flour
- 1/4 cup cornmeal
- Cornmeal to dust sheet pan

In a large mixing bowl, combine soy milk, sugar, yeast, and salt. Stir well and allow to sit 5 to 10 minutes. Blend in oil, then flours and cornmeal. Stir together well and knead for at least 3 minutes in bread mixer or by hand on floured surface. Place in bowl covered loosely with plastic wrap and allow to rise in warm place (75° to 80°F) until nearly doubled in size, approximately 30 to 40 minutes.

Preheat oven to 350°F.

Grease sheet pan and lightly dust with cornmeal. Punch down dough and divide into 6 balls of equal size. Form balls into disks. Rotating each disk in hands, gently tuck the edges of each disk under and toward the center of bottom, slightly stretching top to a smooth tightness. Place on sheet pan and flatten until approximately 1 inch thick and 4 inches wide. Allow to rise for a few minutes in warm place (75° to 80°F) until nearly doubled in size. Bake on middle oven rack for 20 to 30 minutes until browned on bottom. May be further browned on top by placing very briefly under broiler. Remove to a wire rack and cool completely.

Yields 6 large buns.

Breads

Grit Cornbread

2 cups yellow cornmeal

2 cups all-purpose flour

I tablespoon plus I teaspoon
double-acting baking powder

I teaspoon baking soda

I tablespoon sugar

I teaspoon salt

2 large eggs

2-1/2 cups buttermilk

6 tablespoons melted butter

1/2 cup shredded carrots

1/2 cup shredded red cabbage

I cup fresh cooked or frozen corn

1/2 cup shredded mild cheddar
cheese

Preheat oven to 425°F. Grease a 9 x 13-inch metal baking pan.

Whisk together cornmeal, flour, baking powder, baking soda, sugar, and salt in a large mixing bowl. Beat together eggs, buttermilk, and melted butter and add to cornmeal mixture, stirring just until blended. Add vegetables and cheese and stir just until combined. Spread evenly in prepared pan. Bake for 35 minutes or until a knife or toothpick inserted in center comes out clean. Cool for 15 minutes in pan on a wire rack. Cut into squares.

Yields 12 servings.

Excellent sliced through the center of each square and toasted or buttered and browned in skillet.

"I eat at The Grit every time I visit Athens, without fail. In my opinion, The Grit is quite simply the best vegetarian restaurant in the country (and I believe I've tried most of them)."

—JOHN STROHM, BLAKE BABIES

Irish Soda Bread

Serve a thick, toasted slice with soup or with jam for breakfast. Its combination of savory and sweet flavors will have you sneaking back to the kitchen for one more nibble.

2 cups all-purpose flour
1 cup whole wheat flour
3 tablespoons packed light brown sugar
1-1/4 teaspoon salt
2 teaspoons double-acting baking powder
1 teaspoon baking soda
2 tablespoons caraway seeds
4 tablespoons cold butter
2 cups raisins, craisins, or a blend of both, finely minced
1 large egg
1-1/2 cups buttermilk

Preheat oven to 350°F. Grease a baking sheet.

Thoroughly combine flours, sugar, salt, baking powder, baking soda, and caraway seeds. With pastry blender, cut in butter until finely blended and stir in minced raisins and/or craisins.

In a small bowl, beat egg together with buttermilk. Add to flour mixture. Gently stir and fold until just combined. Form dough into a rounded, disk-shaped loaf a few inches thick and 7 to 8 inches wide. Place on prepared baking sheet. Using a sharp knife, mark top of loaf decoratively with 1/2-inch deep knife slashes. Bake on middle oven rack for 1 hour or until a knife or toothpick inserted in center comes out clean. Remove to a wire rack and cool completely.

Yields 1 loaf or 10 servings.

Freezes well for later use.

Breads

Breads

Foxy's Beer Bread

What beer is best? We like Blue Moon White Ale (it's hearty yet tangy), but try your favorite in this fast and easy recipe.

> 2-1/2 cups all-purpose flour
> 3 tablespoons sugar
> 2-1/2 teaspoons baking powder
> 1/2 teaspoon baking soda
> 1/2 teaspoon salt
> 1/2 teaspoon dried oregano
> 1/4 teaspoon dried marjoram
> 1/4 teaspoon dried thyme
> 1 (12-ounce) beer (the heartier, the better)
> 1-1/2 cups shredded white cheddar or mozzarella cheese
> 1 jalapeño pepper, very finely chopped

Preheat oven to 375°F. Grease a 9 x 13-inch pan or glass baking dish.

Sift together the first 8 (dry) ingredients in a large mixing bowl. Add the remaining ingredients and stir just until fully combined. Spread batter evenly into baking pan or dish. Bake for approximately 35 minutes or until a clean knife or toothpick inserted into center of bread comes out clean. Cool in pan for at least 15 minutes, cut, and serve. It's excellent served with butter.

Yields 12 servings.

Cinnamon Raisin–Craisin Bread

Breads

Slice it thick, toast it well.

1-1/4 cups very warm (105°F max) water

1 tablespoon fast-rising dry yeast

1/4 cup packed light brown sugar

1 cup whole wheat flour

6 tablespoons (3/4 stick) butter

1 teaspoon plus a pinch salt

1/4 cup honey

1 teaspoon plus a pinch cinnamon

1 teaspoon pure vanilla extract

2 teaspoons freshly squeezed lemon juice

1/4 cup crushed walnuts

1-1/2 cups raisins, craisins, or blend of both

2-1/2 cups all-purpose flour

Thoroughly combine water, yeast, sugar, and whole wheat flour in a large bowl. Cover loosely with plastic wrap. Allow to sit in a warm place (75° to 80°F) for 20 to 30 minutes.

Melt butter and pour into a small bowl. Add remaining ingredients except all-purpose flour. Allow to cool. Combine butter mixture with yeast mixture and add all-purpose flour. Knead vigorously with mixer or by hand on floured surface for 3 to 4 minutes. Cover bowl loosely with plastic wrap and allow to rise in warm place (75° to 80°F) until nearly doubled in size.

Preheat oven to 375°F. Grease an 8-1/2 x 4-1/2-inch (6 cup) loaf pan.

Punch down dough and form into loaf, gently tucking dough toward center of bottom and lightly stretching the top to a smooth tightness; allow to rise 5 minutes. Place in prepared loaf pan. Bake on middle oven rack for 35 minutes or until nicely browned and hollow-sounding when tapped on bottom. Cool for 10 minutes in pan then remove bread to a wire rack to cool completely. Serve sliced and toasted.

Yields 1 loaf or 8 servings.

Freezes well for later use.

"My favorite thing about The Grit is that the menu is so expansive and that it is frequented by truly nice and interesting people. One of my favorite restaurants in the country."

—AMBER VALENTINE,
JUCIFER

"I love the healthy and exquisite food after a long run of truck-stop fare, and the cute waitresses are easy on the eyes. Sort of a Hooters for the indie rock set. Oops—was that out loud?"

—JOHNNY HICKMAN, CRACKER

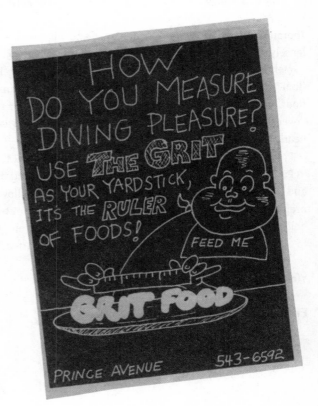

sandwiches

Lunch at The Grit is usually a big ol' sandwich with some soup, chips, or coleslaw. Come prepared for an escapade of meatless wizardry, compliments of the folks who make our specials, or try some of their magic in your own kitchen.

- Herbie's Cream Cheese Spread
- Hummus Pita
- Tofu Bacon and Avocado Sandwich
- Tofu Reuben
- Chicken Salad-Style Tofu Sandwich
- Philly Cheese "Steak" Sandwich
- Spicy Honey BBQ Tofu Sandwich
- Sunday Miracle BBQ Sandwich

Rosa's Bagel

Top a toasted bagel with ripe fresh tomato slices, shredded mild white cheddar cheese, and a pinch of fresh or dried parsley, basil, and oregano. Melt cheese under a broiler and drizzle generously with **Grit Vinaigrette**.

The Smelt

Essentially a glorified grilled cheese sandwich . . . but glorified by delicious **Ted Bread** and our **Honey Mustard Dressing**!

Melt a generous amount of shredded mild white cheddar cheese on two thick slices of **Ted Bread**. Add ripe tomato slices and/or fresh spinach. Top with **Honey Mustard Dressing**. Assemble sandwich and brown both sides in a buttered heavy skillet.

Herbie's Cream Cheese Spread

2 (8-ounce) blocks regular (not whipped or low-fat) cream cheese, softened
3 small green onions (green parts only), minced
2 tablespoons minced fresh parsley or 2 teaspoons dried
2 tablespoons chopped fresh basil or 2 teaspoons dried
1 tablespoon minced fresh dill or 2 teaspoons dried
1 teaspoon minced fresh garlic
1/4 teaspoon plus a pinch salt
Pinch of white pepper
8 slices of bread or 4 toasted bagels
Shredded cabbage, cucumbers, and carrots

Cut cream cheese into small cubes, place in food processor with remaining ingredients, and blend to creamy smoothness. Cover and refrigerate at least 1 hour. Serve cool on bread or toasted bagel with shredded vegetables.

Yields 2-1/2 cups or enough for 4 sandwiches.

This spread is also great served as an appetizer with crackers or crispy cut vegetables. It keeps up to 5 days in the refrigerator.

Hummus Pita Ⓥ

You can also enjoy this classic Middle Eastern dip with crackers or crispy cut vegetables as an appetizer. Do they call 'em chickpeas 'cause they look like little chickens?

- 2 (15.5-ounce) cans chickpeas (garbanzo beans), drained, with liquid reserved
- 1/2 medium red onion, finely chopped
- 2 scant teaspoons cumin powder
- 3/4 teaspoon freshly ground black pepper

- 3/4 teaspoon salt
- 1/2 cup freshly squeezed lemon juice
- 1/4 cup extra-virgin olive oil
- 1/2 to 3/4 teaspoon minced fresh garlic
- 1/3 cup tahini (sesame seed paste)

Puree all ingredients except chickpea liquid in food processor. Gradually add the minimum amount of chickpea liquid required to give the mixture a thick, creamy, smooth consistency. Blend until all graininess is gone. Cover and refrigerate at least 1 hour. Serve cool in pitas sliced in half with shredded cabbage, cucumbers, and carrots.

Yields approximately 4 cups or enough for 6 sandwiches.

Hummus will keep up to 3 days in the refrigerator.

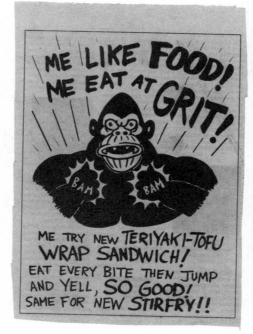

ME LIKE FOOD! ME EAT AT GRIT!

BAM BAM

ME TRY NEW TERIYAKI-TOFU WRAP SANDWICH! EAT EVERY BITE THEN JUMP AND YELL, SO GOOD! SAME FOR NEW STIRFRY!!

Teriyaki Tofu Wrap Sandwich

Sauté cubed tofu in a generous amount of our **Teriyaki Sauce**. Drain and sauté again with your choice of shredded vegetables in the manner of a stir-fry. Roll up in a warm piece of pita bread. Wrap in foil for handling.

Tofu and Avocado Vinaigrette Wrap

Roll up **Grit-Style Tofu** and avocado in a warm flour tortilla with a small handful of mild shredded cheddar cheese and a light drizzling of **Grit Vinaigrette**. Wrap in foil for handling.

Sandwiches

Tofu Bacon and Avocado Sandwich V

It's crispy, sweet, and smoky! Sizzle up our tofu bacon for a T.L.T. or simply as a brunch side dish.

1/2 cup soy sauce
1/8 scant teaspoon liquid smoke
Large pinch freshly ground black pepper
Large pinch sugar or 1/2 teaspoon pure maple syrup
1 (15-ounce) block firm tofu
Vegetable oil
4 slices of bread
1 ripe avocado, peeled and sliced

Blend soy sauce, liquid smoke, pepper, and sugar or syrup; set aside.

Place tofu on cutting board broad side down and cut into quarters. Thinly slice each section lengthwise.

Heavily oil a large, non-stick skillet and place over high heat. When oil is hot, add half of sliced tofu. Toss with a non-metal spatula until tofu begins to brown. Gradually add half of soy mixture and cook until tofu is crispy and sauce is caramelized. Remove from pan; set aside.

Wipe or rinse pan, and repeat process for second half of batch.

Divide tofu bacon between 2 slices of bread, top with 1/2 of the avocado and the remaining slices of bread. Serve immediately.

Yields 2 sandwiches.

Tofu Reuben

1 (15-ounce) block firm tofu
2 tablespoons olive oil
Dash of liquid smoke
1/3 cup soy sauce
1 teaspoon freshly squeezed lemon juice
1/4 teaspoon dried dill
1/4 teaspoon paprika
1/4 teaspoon granulated garlic
4 slices rye bread, toasted
Shredded Swiss cheese
Sauerkraut
Russian dressing

Place tofu broad-side down and cut into quarters. Thinly slice each quarter. In a large non-stick skillet, heat olive oil over medium-high heat. Add tofu. Toss and turn frequently until tofu begins to brown.

Combine a dash of liquid smoke with soy sauce, and add mixture to tofu with remaining spices. Toss to brown evenly and sauté until tofu is very firm and slightly browned. Serve on rye bread with shredded Swiss cheese, sauerkraut, and Russian dressing.

Yields 2 large sandwiches.

Sandwiches

Sandwiches

Chicken Salad-Style Tofu Sandwich

We proudly serve this as a sandwich on our **Ted Bread**, and it goes fast! It satisfies the meat eaters and leaves the vegetarians confident that they ain't missing a thing. It also uses up your leftover **Golden Bowl** (not that there usually *is* any left over), and that last little bit of your **Grit Vinaigrette**.

2-1/2 cups Grit-Style Tofu (prepared at least 6 hours to a day before)
1/4 cup Grit Yeast Gravy
1/2 cup finely minced red onion
1/2 cup finely chopped celery
Freshly squeezed juice of I lemon
1/2 cup mayonnaise
1/4 cup **Grit Vinaigrette**, plus more for dressing sandwiches
1/2 teaspoon sugar
1/4 teaspoon salt
1/4 teaspoon hot sauce
1/4 teaspoon Dijon mustard
1/4 generous teaspoon curry powder
1/4 teaspoon freshly ground black pepper
Large pinch granulated garlic
10 to 12 toasted whole wheat bread slices
Lettuce leaves
I ripe medium tomato, sliced

Marinate tofu in just enough gravy to coat it, and refrigerate at least 6 hours. Don't worry, it's worth it.

With a large knife, chop tofu into random pieces resembling chunks of chopped, cooked chicken breast. (A variety of sizes is key to a convincing imitation of chicken consistency, so do not use a food processor.) Combine tofu with remaining ingredients and chill at least I hour. Assemble sandwiches on toasted bread with lettuce, tomato, and a touch more **Grit Vinaigrette**.

Yields 2-1/2 to 3 cups or enough for 5 or 6 sandwiches.

Philly Cheese "Steak" Sandwich

Sandwiches

The sandwich with a fan club.

- 1 cup chunky beef-style T.V.P. (textured vegetable protein)
- 1-2/3 cups water
- 1 tablespoon olive oil
- 1 small or 1/2 large onion, cut into thin crescents
- 1 small green bell pepper, seeded and thinly sliced
- 1 tablespoon vegan Worcestershire sauce
- 2 large hoagie rolls
- Mayonnaise
- Shredded Swiss or mild white cheddar cheese
- Red or green leaf lettuce
- 1/2 ripe medium tomato, sliced

Combine T.V.P. and water in a saucepan and bring to a boil; set aside.

In a heavy skillet, heat olive oil. Add onion and pepper and sauté until soft. Drain T.V.P. and add to vegetables with Worcestershire sauce. Sauté briefly until vegetables are well done and T.V.P. slightly browned. Serve warm on a hoagie roll with mayonnaise, shredded cheese, lettuce, and tomato.

Yields 2 sandwiches.

Sandwiches

Spicy Honey BBQ Tofu Sandwich (V)

1-1/2 (15-ounce) block firm tofu
Vegetable oil
1/2 cup soy sauce
1 small or 1/2 large yellow onion, finely minced
1 teaspoon minced garlic
1/4 teaspoon freshly ground black pepper
1/2 teaspoon dry mustard
1/4 teaspoon fennel seed or 1/8 teaspoon ground fennel
Pinch of dried ginger
Pinch of fresh chopped or dried thyme
Pinch of cayenne pepper
Pinch of freshly ground cinnamon
1 cup ketchup
3/4 cup freshly squeezed orange juice
1/2 cup honey
2 tablespoons cider vinegar
4 onion rolls
Lettuce leaves
1 ripe medium tomato, sliced

Tear tofu by hand into chunks of various sizes. Lightly coat the inside of a large non-stick skillet with oil and place over high heat. Sauté tofu, tossing often until it begins to brown. Gradually add soy sauce and sauté briefly until tofu is lightly crispy on exterior but tender inside; set aside.

Lightly coat the inside of a large saucepan with oil and place over high heat. Add onions and garlic; when they are hot, stir in black pepper, dry mustard, spices, and herbs. Sauté until onions are brown, approximately 5 minutes. Stir in ketchup, orange juice, honey, and vinegar. Bring mixture barely to a boil, stirring often, and add prepared tofu. Cook until tofu is warmed through and sauce thickens. Remove from heat. Serve on toasted onion rolls with lettuce and tomato.

Yields 4 sandwiches.

Sunday Miracle BBQ Sandwich

Served Sunday evenings at The Grit on an **Old-Time Grit Bun** with slaw or corn on the cob. The secret is to brown the bejesus out of the tempeh. The miracle is *it ain't meat!*

3 (8-ounce) packages tempeh
Vegetable oil or butter
4 tablespoons butter or vegan
   margarine
1 large yellow onion, finely chopped
1 tablespoon minced fresh garlic
1 tablespoon dry mustard
2 teaspoons curry powder
1 teaspoon onion powder
1/4 teaspoon freshly ground black
   pepper
Generous pinch cayenne pepper
2 cups strong brewed coffee
3 cups ketchup

1 cup apple juice
1/2 cup cider vinegar
1/2 cup soy sauce
4 tablespoons vegan Worcestershire
   sauce
4 tablespoons pineapple or orange-
   pineapple juice concentrate (or
   1 cup finely chopped fresh or
   canned crushed pineapple, in juice)
1 cup grated carrot
5 medium green onions (dark green
   parts only), minced
6 toasted **Old-Time Grit Buns**

Slice tempeh into strips 2 inches long and 1/4- to 1/2-inch thick. In a small amount of vegetable oil or butter in a medium saucepan, sauté tempeh, tossing often to cook evenly, until extremely well browned; set aside.

Melt 4 tablespoons butter or margarine in a large pot and add onion and garlic. Cook over high heat, stirring often, until caramelized. Stir in seasonings and cook briefly, then add all remaining ingredients except tempeh, carrots, and green onions. Bring mixture to a boil and cook, stirring often, until it thickens. Stir in prepared tempeh, carrots, and green onions. Cook over medium-high heat, stirring often, for 4 or 5 minutes. Remove from heat and allow to sit for 10 minutes before serving on a toasted bun.

Yields 6 sandwiches.

Makes an excellent side dish when served over steamed rice. Yields 8 servings.

Sandwiches

"When I am home I eat at The Grit, when I am away I look forward to being home so I can eat at The Grit. Rarely do you see the same special twice, although you often wish you could."

—BERTIS DOWNS, R.E.M. MANAGER

KING OF FOOD

Flame On

"If every town had a vegetarian restaurant as good as The Grit there would be a lot more cows, pigs, and chickens running around."

—DAVE SCHOOLS, WIDESPREAD PANIC

entrées

Here is a variety of meatless main courses that satisfy even big appetites without relying on mountains of melted cheese. Many of these dishes are regular specials at The Grit and a few have achieved cult status. Perhaps the only customer frustration with Grit specials is not knowing exactly which night a favorite like **Tofu "Meatloaf"** might appear again. Now it can appear whenever you want, along with other heavy-hitters that go a long way towards giving vegetarian entrées a good name.

- **Pasta Entrées**
- **Tofu Entrées**
- **One Great Seitan Entrée**
- **Quesadillas, One Mondo Burrito, and a Casserole**

Linguine with Smoked Gouda and Wine Sauce

2 vegetarian "sausage" links, chopped into small pieces
1 tablespoon olive oil
3 tablespoons butter
1 small yellow onion, finely chopped
1 small green bell pepper, finely chopped
2 cups trimmed and sliced button or cremini mushrooms
1/4 cup all-purpose flour
1 teaspoon salt
1 teaspoon white pepper
2 cups whole milk
2 cups shredded smoked Gouda cheese
1 cup shredded mild cheddar cheese
1 cup dry white wine
1/2 cup heavy cream
3 tablespoons minced fresh basil or rosemary
1/2 cup freshly grated Parmesan cheese
16 ounces linguine, freshly cooked

Sauté sausage pieces in olive oil until well browned; set aside.

Melt butter in a large pot and add onion and bell pepper. Sauté until onion is translucent. Add mushrooms and sauté until mushrooms are well done. Add flour, salt, and pepper and cook over gentle heat for 5 minutes, stirring often. Gradually stir in milk and adjust heat to bring mixture to a gentle boil.

Stir in Gouda and cheddar cheeses. When cheeses are fully melted, add wine and heavy cream. Cook over gentle heat for 10 minutes, stirring often. Add prepared sausages and basil or rosemary and cook for 5 minutes, continuing to stir frequently. Remove from heat and blend in Parmesan cheese. Serve over pasta.

Yields 5 or 6 servings.

Spinach Fettucine with Cajun Alfredo Sauce

Pasta Entrées

4 tablespoons butter
2 vegetarian "sausage" links, finely chopped
2 cups trimmed and sliced button or cremini mushrooms
4 cups heavy cream
1 tablespoon paprika
1/2 teaspoon salt
1/4 scant teaspoon cayenne pepper
1/4 teaspoon dry mustard
1/4 teaspoon ground sage
1 scant teaspoon chopped fresh thyme or 1/4 teaspoon dried
1 cup freshly grated Parmesan cheese
16 ounces dried spinach fettucine, freshly cooked

In a large pot, melt butter and add "sausage" and mushrooms. Sauté until both are well browned, approximately 7 to 10 minutes.

Add remaining ingredients except Parmesan cheese. Stirring often, bring mixture to a gentle boil and cook until sauce thickens. Remove from heat and stir in Parmesan cheese. Serve immediately over spinach fettucine.

Yields 5 to 6 servings.

"The Grit's mushrooms: delightful, tasteful, and introspective."
—CHET WEISE, THE QUADRAJETS

Pasta Entrées

Spinach and Feta Lasagna

8 ounces lasagna noodles, freshly cooked
4 quarts water
1/2 (15-ounce) block firm tofu, crumbled
1 teaspoon soy sauce
1/2 teaspoon dry mustard
1/4 teaspoon freshly ground black pepper
1-1/2 cups crumbled feta cheese
1 pound frozen spinach, thawed and drained
4 cups Grit Marinara
4 cups shredded mozzarella cheese (preferably fresh)
3/4 cup freshly grated Parmesan cheese
2 teaspoons mixture of dried parsley, oregano, and basil

Preheat oven to 350°F. Oil a 9 x 13-inch baking dish.

Boil lasagna noodles in 4 quarts water until barely tender. Drain and separate the noodles; set aside.

Combine tofu, soy sauce, mustard, pepper, feta cheese, and spinach in a large mixing bowl.

Lightly coat bottom of prepared pan with marinara. Cover the sauce with a layer of pasta running the length of the pan and overlapping the noodles by 1/2 inch. Spread with 1/2 of the spinach-feta mixture, 1/3 of the marinara, and 1/2 of the mozzarella cheese. Cover with a second equal layer of all ingredients, but with the second layer of noodles laying perpendicular to the first. Cover with a third layer of noodles running the length of the pan and top with the remaining marinara. Sprinkle with Parmesan cheese and parsley. Bake for 40 to 50 minutes or until well browned on top. Cool slightly before serving.

Yields 6 large or 10 small servings.

Tempeh Tetrazzini with White Wine Cream Sauce

Pasta Entrées

A creamy, delicious casserole with a few extra steps . . . and the flavor to elicit "oohs" and "aahs" (while showcasing tempeh at its tastiest). Serve with a salad to balance the richness. Preparation is divided into component sections.

The Sauce

6 tablespoons butter (3/4 stick)	I tablespoon soy sauce
6 tablespoons white flour	I generous teaspoon salt
4-1/4 cups milk, divided	1/4 teaspoon dry or prepared
1/4 cup white wine	mustard
I tablespoon Worcestershire sauce	1/8 teaspoon black pepper

To prepare sauce: This section requires a bit of technique, so please read it carefully before beginning.

In a 2-quart, heavy-bottomed saucepan, melt butter, being careful not to brown it. Stir in white flour until blended, over just enough heat to make mixture bubble. Stir or whisk almost constantly to avoid lumping or burning. Still using only enough heat to maintain vigorous bubbling without browning mixture, deeply stir or whisk almost constantly for approximately 3-1/2 minutes. This is the amount of time required to cook the flour to smoothness, and vigorous and thorough whisking of the mixture, or roux, is important to avoid burning or browning.

Raise heat and gradually whisk in 2 cups of milk. Be prepared for the mixture to rapidly become thick and custard-like. As ingredients are whisked in, try to strike a balance between heat level and speed of liquid additions, maintaining a consistency of thick sauce, just hot enough to bubble slightly.

Whisk in all remaining ingredients except for remaining 2-1/4 cups milk. When mixture achieves thick consistency again, gradually whisk in remaining milk at a slow pace. Maintain some thickness, and cook until bubbling well and re-thickened. Remove from heat and set aside.

Pasta Entrées

The Tempeh

2 tablespoons butter
3/4 cup finely chopped onion
1 teaspoon minced garlic or 1/4
teaspoon garlic powder
1 (8-ounce) package soy tempeh,
chopped into 1/2-inch cubes

2 tablespoons soy sauce
2 tablespoons Worcestershire sauce
2 tablespoons water
1 cup finely chopped mushrooms

To prepare tempeh: In a large skillet over medium-high heat, melt butter and add onions and garlic. Sauté at a sizzle for approximately 2 minutes or until onions are translucent. Add tempeh and combine well with onions. Sprinkle on soy sauce and Worcestershire sauce and distribute well, tossing and stirring tempeh and onions to brown evenly. Add water as needed to avoid burning. Sauté approximately 2 minutes. Stir in mushrooms and continue to stir and sauté until mushrooms are tender and tempeh is deeply browned. Remove from heat and set aside.

The Vegetables

1-1/4 cups coined baby carrots or
finely chopped carrots

1-1/2 cups finely chopped celery
1-1/4 cups frozen green peas

To prepare vegetables: Bring 2 quarts of water to a boil. Add carrots and boil for approximately 2 minutes. Add celery and boil until carrots and celery are tender but not fully softened, approximately 3 more minutes. Throw in green peas, then immediately drain and set aside.

The Noodles, the Cheese, and the Breadcrumbs

Egg noodles, enough to yield 4 cups
cooked
2 cups shredded white cheddar,
mozzarella, or other mild
white cheese

1 generous cup breadcrumbs
(see page 79)
1 tablespoon grated Parmesan
cheese (optional)

To prepare noodles, cheese, and breadcrumbs: Choose your favorite egg noodle pasta and prepare per package instructions. Cook until al dente. Drain well.

Shred enough cheese to yield 2 cups. To add an exciting twist, add a smoked cheese to the mix.

Grind enough breadcrumbs finely in a food processor to yield 1 generous cup. If desired, blend in a tablespoon of grated Parmesan cheese.

To assemble Tempeh Tetrazzini: Once all components (cream sauce, tempeh, vegetables, pasta, cheese, and breadcrumbs) are prepared, preheat oven to 375° F . Grease a 9 x 13-inch pan or glass casserole dish. Cover bottom of pan or dish evenly with about 1 cup of cream sauce. Distribute one-half of tempeh mixture evenly over sauce. Continue to evenly distribute ingredients in layers in this order:

    1 cup shredded cheese
    1 cup carrot mixture
    4 cups pasta
    2 cups cream sauce
    remaining half of tempeh mixture
    remaining carrot mixture
    remaining cup of shredded cheese
    remaining cream sauce
    1 cup breadcrumbs

Lightly press down on crumbs to compact crust. Place in oven and bake for 40 minutes or until edges are bubbling vigorously and crumb topping is very well browned. Allow to cool and set briefly before serving.

Yields 6 generous servings.

Pasta Entrées

Pasta Entrées

Jimmy Ray's Herbed Dumplings

These tender bits of heaven are a perfect entrée for a cold winter's night with friends and family. Serve them with **Butternut Cream Sauce** or **Caramelized Onion and Red Wine Brown Sauce**. Here we offer two equally scrumptious options: one with dairy and one without.

3 quarts vegetable stock	1/2 teaspoon dried rosemary
4 cups white flour	1/4 teaspoon garlic powder
4 tablespoons baking powder	1/4 teaspoon onion powder
2 teaspoons salt	6 tablespoons (3/4 stick) butter or
1 teaspoon thyme	vegan margarine for dairy-free
1 teaspoon dried parsley or 1	version
tablespoon fresh parsley	4 cups milk or soy milk for dairy-free
1 teaspoon dried sage	version
1/2 teaspoon dried oregano	

Place vegetable stock in a large stockpot over high heat to boil. As it is heating, assemble dumplings as follows.

Sift together the 10 dry ingredients in a large bowl and set aside.

Place butter or margarine and milk or soy milk in a saucepan and heat just until simmering. Remove mixture from heat and pour into the bowl containing the dry ingredients. Gently blend mixture with a spoon until thoroughly and uniformly combined.

As vegetable stock reaches a full boil, form dumpling mixture into balls just under 2 inches in diameter. Place the dumplings gently into the boiling stock. Boil for approximately 10 minutes. Dumplings will nearly double in size. Use a slotted spoon to remove dumplings and serve immediately, drizzled with the sauce of your choice.

Yields 4 servings.

Tofu "Meatloaf"

2 tablespoons olive oil
1 small yellow onion, finely minced
1 teaspoon minced fresh garlic
1 small green bell pepper, finely minced
2 cups vegetarian ground "beef"
2 tablespoons vegan Worcestershire sauce
1 (15-ounce) block firm tofu, crumbled
1 cup quick-cooking rolled oats
1 cup walnut pieces

4 tablespoons ketchup
1/2 cup nutritional yeast
1/2 cup soy sauce
1 teaspoon paprika
1/2 teaspoon salt
1/2 teaspoon freshly ground black pepper
1-1/2 teaspoon chopped fresh rosemary or 1/2 teaspoon dried
1/2 teaspoon onion powder
1/2 teaspoon dry mustard

Preheat oven to 350°F. Grease a shallow baking pan.

Heat olive oil in a large skillet and add onions, garlic, and peppers. Sauté until translucent, stirring often. Add vegetarian ground "beef" and Worcestershire sauce. Cook on low heat, stirring often, for 20 minutes.

In a food processor, combine remaining ingredients and process until fully blended. Combine all ingredients and mix well. Form mixture into 3 or 4 loaves 1 inch thick and place in prepared pan. Bake on middle oven rack for 20 minutes. Turn over and bake an additional 20 minutes, or until each side is well browned. Cool on a wire rack for 5 minutes before serving.

Yields 3 or 4 servings.

Excellent served with a side of mashed potatoes and smothered with Sage and Onion Gravy.

Tofu Entrées

- **Tofu "Meatloaf"**
- **Tofu Parmesan**
- **Thai Tofu Tacos**
- **Jerk Tofu**
- **Sweet-and-Sour Tofu and Vegetables**
- **Cashew Coconut Cream Curry**
- **Tofu Wellington**
- **General Chin's 5-Star Tofu Delight**

Tofu Entrées

Tofu Parmesan

3 (15-ounce) blocks tofu, firm or
  extra-firm
2 tablespoons olive oil
Soy sauce
2 large eggs, beaten
1-1/2 cups freshly grated Parmesan
  cheese, plus more for garnish
1 tablespoon chopped fresh parsley
  or 1 generous teaspoon dried, plus
  more for garnish

2-1/2 cups fine breadcrumbs
1/2 teaspoon salt
1/8 teaspoon freshly ground black
  pepper
4 cups Grit Marinara
2 cups shredded mozzarella cheese
  (preferably fresh)
Chopped fresh or dried oregano, for
  garnish

Preheat oven to 375°F. Grease a 9 x 13-inch baking pan or glass casserole dish.

Tear tofu by hand into chunks of various sizes. Add a thin layer of olive oil to a non-stick skillet and place over high heat. Cover bottom of pan with tofu chunks and sauté, tossing often and sprinkling with soy sauce, until tofu is very firm and somewhat crispy; set aside. Repeat with another small batch of tofu until all of tofu is cooked in this manner. Drain tofu if necessary and cool slightly. Place in a bowl with beaten eggs and toss together.

Blend 1-1/2 cups Parmesan cheese, parsley, breadcrumbs, salt, and pepper. Add to tofu and toss together.

Pour 2 cups marinara into prepared pan and spread evenly. Distribute tofu over sauce. Bake for 25 to 30 minutes or until tofu breading is very well browned. Remove from oven and spread top with 2 cups marinara sauce and mozzarella cheese. Garnish with remaining Parmesan cheese, parsley, and oregano. Return to oven and bake 10 to 15 minutes until top is well browned.

Yields 8 to 10 servings.

Thai Tofu Tacos

1-1/2 (15-ounce) blocks firm tofu, crumbled
4 tablespoons vegetable oil, divided
4 tablespoons soy sauce, divided
1/2 small yellow onion, finely chopped
1-1/2 teaspoons minced fresh garlic
1-1/2 teaspoons minced fresh ginger
1/4 teaspoon cumin powder
1/8 teaspoon freshly ground cinnamon
1/8 teaspoon freshly ground nutmeg
1 tablespoon apricot preserves or orange marmalade

1-1/2 teaspoons chili paste
1-1/2 teaspoons packed light brown sugar
1/2 cup smooth peanut butter
1/4 cup tomato puree
1/4 cup coconut milk
2 tablespoons water
4 corn tortillas, warmed
1 cup fresh vegetables, such as shredded carrots, finely chopped romaine lettuce, and/or diced tomatoes

In a non-stick skillet, sauté tofu in 2 tablespoons of oil, stirring often, until golden brown. Sprinkle on 3 tablespoons soy sauce and sauté 1 or 2 minutes; set aside. (It may be necessary to sauté tofu in two batches, depending on skillet size.)

In a large pot over medium-high heat, heat remaining oil. Add onions and sauté until translucent, stirring often. Stir in garlic, ginger, dry spices, preserves or marmalade, chili paste, and sugar. Cook over medium heat for 2 minutes. Stir in peanut butter, tomato puree, coconut milk, water, and 1 tablespoon soy sauce. When mixture is well blended and hot, add prepared tofu and gently simmer, stirring often, for 10 minutes. Remove from heat, cool slightly. Divide equally between corn tortillas, top with fresh vegetables, and serve immediately.

Yields 4 servings.

Breadcrumbs

Place slices of firm-textured, stale whole-wheat bread on an ungreased baking sheet and bake in a warm (about 200°F) oven for an hour or two to completely dry out, but don't let them brown. Grind the dry bread into crumbs with the grating blade of a food processor. Breadcrumbs freeze well.

Tofu Entrées

Jerk Tofu

Great with black beans and rice.

3 green onions (green parts only),
  coarsely chopped
1 small red onion, coarsely chopped
1 tablespoon minced fresh garlic
1 small jalapeño chile, coarsely
  chopped
1 tablespoon minced fresh ginger
1 tablespoon packed light brown
  sugar
1 tablespoon freshly ground allspice
1 tablespoon freshly ground black
  pepper
1 teaspoon freshly ground cinnamon

1 teaspoon cayenne pepper
1 teaspoon freshly ground nutmeg
1 tablespoon chopped fresh thyme
  or 1 teaspoon dried
1 teaspoon salt
1/2 cup freshly squeezed orange juice
1/2 cup rice wine vinegar
1/2 cup red wine vinegar
1/4 cup olive oil
3 (15-ounce) blocks firm tofu
2 tablespoons vegetable oil
1/2 cup soy sauce

In a food processor, combine green onion, red onion, garlic, jalapeño, and ginger and grind into paste. Cover and refrigerate while tofu is prepared.

In a large bowl, combine all remaining ingredients except tofu, vegetable oil, and soy sauce. Whisk together vigorously by hand or with hand mixer until well combined; set aside.

Tear tofu by hand into chunks of various size. In a non-stick skillet, heat vegetable oil over high heat. Sauté tofu until slightly and evenly browned. Sprinkle on soy sauce and sauté 1 or 2 minutes. It may be necessary to sauté tofu in a few batches, depending on skillet size. Combine all ingredients and marinate in refrigerator for 2 hours. Reheat in a non-stick skillet over low heat and serve.

Yields 6 to 8 servings.

Sweet-and-Sour Tofu and Vegetables V

Tofu Entrées

Sauce:
1/2 cup honey
1 cup finely chopped fresh pineapple or 1 cup crushed canned pineapple, in juice
1/2 cup soy sauce
1/2 cup cider vinegar
6 tablespoons ketchup
4 tablespoons rice wine vinegar
3 tablespoons freshly squeezed lemon juice
1/2 teaspoon fresh minced garlic
1/2 teaspoon onion powder
1 cup water
2 tablespoons cornstarch

Tofu and Vegetables:
2 (15-ounce) blocks firm silken tofu
Vegetable oil
Soy sauce
2 carrots, peeled and thinly julienned
1 broccoli crown, broken or cut into small florets
1/2 green bell pepper, cut into thin strips
1/2 red bell pepper, cut into thin strips
1 small or 1/2 large onion, finely minced or cut into thin crescents
16 ounces dried Asian egg noodles, freshly cooked, or 2 cups rice, steamed

To prepare sauce: Combine all ingredients except water and cornstarch in a saucepan and bring to a boil. Blend water and cornstarch, then stir into boiling sauce. Cook until thickened slightly and remove from heat.

To prepare tofu and vegetables: Slice each tofu block in half to yield 4 broad, flat slabs. Press tofu slabs between 2 flat pans and place a heavy object, such as a stack of plates or canned goods, on top pan. Leave for 15 to 20 minutes until all liquid is removed, then drain and discard liquid.

Slice tofu into pieces approximately 2 x 1/2 inches. In a non-stick skillet or wok with a minimal amount of vegetable oil, lightly sauté tofu over medium-high heat for 5 minutes. Sprinkle lightly with soy sauce as tofu cooks. Brown lightly; set aside.

Sauté vegetables, peppers, and onion in the same manner, using minimal oil and sprinkling lightly with soy sauce, over enough heat to tenderize and somewhat sear vegetables without making them soggy or dull in color, about 3 minutes.

Return tofu to skillet or wok and stir to mix with vegetables, then add sauce and toss to cover completely. Serve over noodles or rice.

Yields 8 servings.

Tofu Entrées

Cashew Coconut Cream Curry

Rich, creamy and spicy . . . brightened by fresh vegetables and a touch of fresh lemon . . . easy and rewarding, once you round up some cashew butter, coconut milk, and hot chili sauce.

2-1/2 cups vegetarian "chicken" broth (available at most natural foods stores)
3/4 cup chopped baby carrots
1-1/2 cups chopped broccoli
3/4 cup sliced mushrooms
1/2 cup frozen green peas, thawed
1/4 cup cashew butter
1/2 to 2/3 cup coconut milk (depending on taste)
1 tablespoon soy or tamari sauce (plus an additional teaspoon if desired)

1 teaspoon hot chili sauce (or to taste)
1 teaspoon fresh lemon juice
1/4 to 1/2 teaspoon curry powder (depending on taste)
1 (8-ounce) package baked, seasoned tofu (available at most natural food stores)
cashews for garnish (optional)

In a large stockpot over high heat, bring vegetarian "chicken" broth to a gentle boil. Add carrots and boil for 2 minutes. Add broccoli and boil for 2 minutes. Add mushrooms and green peas and boil approximately 1 minute. Reduce heat to medium.

Thoroughly blend in cashew butter, then stir in all remaining ingredients except baked tofu. Bear in mind that the saltiness of vegetarian "chicken" broth might vary from brand to brand, and adjusting the amount of soy or tamari sauce will allow control over sodium content and flavor. Continue cooking and frequently stirring at a simmer while preparing tofu by cutting or shredding by hand into chunks of desired size. Stir in tofu and simmer briefly. Taste result and adjust seasonings if desired.

This curry is delicious on its own or over rice or noodles (increased seasonings are recommended if serving over a starch). If desired, garnish with crumbled cashews.

Yields 4 (large) or 5 servings.

Tofu Wellington

This recipe yields 3 marinated tofu cutlets, surrounded with rich mushroom pâté, which are wrapped in phyllo pastry and baked to a golden brown. This hearty vegetarian version of a culinary classic involves several steps, but the result is well worth the effort. Traditionally served with **Brown Sauce**, it also goes nicely with **Butternut Squash Cream Sauce** or **Sage and Onion Gravy**. Please begin by defrosting a package of phyllo pastry.

The Tofu

1/2 cup soy sauce	1/4 teaspoon liquid smoke
4 tablespoons maple syrup	1 dash black pepper
1 tablespoon Worcestershire sauce (vegetarian)	1 block of tofu sliced to yield three 3 x 4 x 1/2 inch slabs
1 teaspoon red wine	

Blend all ingredients except tofu to create marinade. Lay tofu slabs on a greased baking sheet. Drizzle lightly with marinade; flip and repeat for other side of tofu and reserve half of marinade for later use. Marinate tofu for at least 30 minutes, flipping periodically to absorb flavor. During this time, preheat oven to 350°F.

Place tofu in oven for 15 minutes, then flip it over and bake for 10 minutes. Drizzle remaining marinade onto both sides and bake for 15 additional minutes. Remove from oven and cool.

The Pâté

3 tablespoons butter or margarine	1-1/2 teaspoon dried thyme
1 tablespoon olive oil	1 teaspoon salt
6 cups (packed) chopped mushrooms	1 teaspoon black pepper
1-1/2 tablespoon minced garlic	1 teaspoon dried oregano
1/2 cup red wine	1 dash white pepper
1/4 cup nutritional yeast	

Tofu Entrées

Tofu Entrées

In a large saucepan, melt butter or margarine with olive oil. Add mushrooms and sauté over medium-high heat until they begin to release moisture. Stir in the garlic and red wine and cook for 5 minutes, stirring occasionally. Blend in all remaining ingredients and cook uncovered, until juices have evaporated and mushrooms darken. Transfer mixture to a food processor and purée until smooth, creamy, and uniform. Set aside to cool.

Tofu Wellington Assembly
1 package phyllo pastry, defrosted for 2 hours
Olive oil or melted butter as needed

Preheat oven to 350°F.

Use a pastry brush to lightly grease a clean, dry food preparation surface with olive oil or melted butter. Lay down a single sheet of phyllo pastry and brush lightly with olive oil or melted butter. Lay another sheet on the first and apply oil or butter. Repeat this until you have a stack of 5 prepared pastry sheets. Place a large, heaping spoonful of mushroom pâté in the center of the top pastry sheet. Place a tofu cutlet on top of the pâté with its rectangular shape oriented in the same way as that of the pastry sheet. Press lightly on the tofu to spread the pâté beneath it and cover the tofu with another spoonful of pâté, reserving enough for all 3 servings. Lift all 5 layers of pastry and fold them over the tofu to neatly envelope it. Place on an ungreased baking sheet, folded side down, and repeat this process for the remaining cutlets.

Drizzle any remaining pastry sheets with oil or butter and tear into strips. Place strips on Wellington portions for decoration. Place Wellingtons in oven and bake for 30 minutes or until pastry is golden brown, and crisp. Carefully remove from baking sheet and serve immediately on a bed of sauce (chosen from our recommendations in the introduction to this recipe).

Tofu Entrées

General Chin's 5-Star Tofu Delight

Jimmy Ray's rendition of a traditional Chinese brown sauce pulls no punches when it comes to the intense flavors of garlic and sesame. Serve this over steamed rice or your favorite Asian noodles.

The Sauce

3/4 cup sesame oil

1 large onion, thinly sliced

3/4 cup minced garlic

3 tablespoons hot chili sauce (we use Sriracha brand) or 2 tablespoons chili paste

2 teaspoons ginger powder

1 teaspoon onion powder

1/2 cup sesame seeds

1 cup orange juice

1 cup sugar

1/2 cup soy sauce

3 tablespoons cornstarch

1 cup water

Heat sesame oil in a large saucepan and add onions. Sauté over medium-high heat, stirring frequently until onions are translucent. Stir in garlic and chili sauce or paste and cook briefly before adding ginger powder, onion powder, and sesame seeds. Stir and cook briefly before adding orange juice, sugar, and soy sauce. Stirring well, bring the mixture to a boil. Blend cornstarch with water and add to boiling mixture, stirring often until it returns to a full boil. When sauce thickens (after 1 to 2 minutes), remove it from heat.

The Tofu and Vegetables

2 blocks firm tofu, well drained

1 cup vegetable oil

1 broccoli crown, cut into medium florets

1 red bell pepper, sliced into thin strips

Slice tofu into 1-inch cubes. Place vegetable oil in a large non-stick frying pan or wok over medium-high heat until hot. Add tofu cubes to hot oil gently to avoid spattering.

Tofu Entrées

Turn heat to high and sauté tofu, turning it often with a wooden or heat-resistant spoon, until evenly golden brown on all sides (if pan capacity is small, sauté tofu in two batches). Remove from heat and carefully drain excess oil. Return pan with tofu to medium heat and add broccoli and red pepper. Sauté for 3 to 5 minutes, until broccoli is bright green. Add the prepared sauce to the pan, stirring to evenly coat vegetables and tofu. Cook for 3 to 4 minutes, stirring well.

Serve immediately over steamed rice or noodles of choice.

Yields 4 servings.

Vegetarian "Beefsteak" (a.k.a. Seitan)

One Great Seitan Entrée

A great vegetarian take on thin-sliced roast beef, this recipe provides the makings for 3 large or 4 decently sized sandwiches (and doubles easily; see note below). Spice it up for hearty quesadillas or try it with **Grit Peanut Sauce** in a vegetable stir-fry and you'll be hooked. Once you find wheat gluten powder at the natural food store, the rest is easy (and worth every step).

If Doubling Recipe: Use 4 quarts of water, with 1 tablespoon salt added, to boil seitan slices. When promptly refrigerated (immersed in water), seitan remains fresh for later use for at least one week.

3 quarts water for boiling	1/2 cup soy sauce
1 teaspoon salt	1/4 teaspoon liquid smoke
3/4 cup water	2-1/2 cups wheat gluten powder
1/2 cup Worcestershire sauce	(available at most natural food
(vegetarian)	stores)

Place 3 quarts of water and 1 teaspoon salt in a stockpot over high heat to boil. As it is heating, blend 3/4 cup water with Worcestershire sauce, soy sauce, and liquid smoke in a large mixing bowl. Add wheat gluten powder and stir until mixture forms a ball. Remove ball from bowl and place on a clean, dry surface. Knead seitan ball by hand as you would bread dough for 2 to 4 minutes, as vigorously and thoroughly as possible.

Using a serrated knife, slice the seitan ball into slabs approximately 1-1/2 inches thick. When the salted water comes to a boil, drop in the slices of seitan one at a time. Stir and lift slices during the first few minutes of boiling so they won't stick to the bottom of the pot and burn. Boil for 15 to 20 minutes, stirring and flipping pieces occasionally. The seitan should float to the surface after about 10 minutes and may need to be pushed down with a utensil to remain submerged. When seitan is fully boiled, remove from heat and place it into cold water to cool. Fully cool and allow to "rest" in refrigerator for at least 1 hour, preferably longer, before further preparation.

One Great Seitan Entrée

From Seitan to "Beefsteak," or the Sauté Phase

The following is a basic recipe for turning prepared seitan into a terrific sandwich, quesadilla, or stir-fry centerpiece . . . with the flavor, look, and aroma of thinly sliced beef sizzled in a spicy marinade. After this, try the exciting variations presented at the end of these instructions.

1 batch of Grit Vegetarian "Beefsteak" (a.k.a. Seitan)	Soy sauce
	Liquid smoke
2 medium-sized yellow onions	1 teaspoon onion powder, divided
Vegetable oil or butter	Hot sauce (optional)
Worcestershire sauce (vegetarian)	Dry or prepared mustard (optional)

Slice seitan as thinly as possible either by hand with a serrated knife or, ideally, by running through a slicing plate in a food processor. Set aside. Peel onions and slice into thin crescents. Place a large skillet or frying pan over medium-high heat. Add oil or butter and, when hot, add onions. Depending on the size of the pan and onions, it may be necessary to divide onions into 2 batches. Sauté onions until translucent, turning frequently. Lightly sprinkle on Worcestershire sauce, soy sauce, and a few drops of liquid smoke. Stir frequently with a spatula to avoid sticking and burning and cook until onions are very soft and caramelized. Remove from pan and set aside.

Clean pan and place over medium-high heat. Add a generous amount of oil or butter. When oil is hot, place a small piece of sliced seitan in the pan. If it sizzles, pan is hot enough. Add half of the sliced seitan. Toss and lift frequently as you sauté.

When the majority of the seitan is somewhat browned, sprinkle on at least 2 tablespoons Worcestershire sauce, 2 tablespoons soy sauce, 2 generous dashes of liquid smoke, plus 1/2 teaspoon of onion powder, tossing and stirring well after each addition to avoid burning. Maintain enough heat to loudly sizzle the seitan. For spicier seitan, increase sauce additions as desired and add small measures of the optional hot sauce and mustard. Adding sauces will accelerate browning. When seitan is deeply brown in color, remove from heat before burning occurs. Remove seitan from pan. Clean the pan and repeat the above process to sauté remaining half of seitan. When done, stir seitan "beefsteak" and onions together to allow flavors to marry before serving with melted cheese of choice on toasted French bread or in quesadillas. Create your own concoction with this hearty, delicious stuff or try one of the Grit's "Beefsteak" specialties such as "Chipotle Cheese Steak Sandwich" or "Seared Beef and Vegetable Stir Fry with Spicy Peanut Sauce" over rice or noodles.

For Chipotle Cheese Steak Sandwich

Follow Vegetarian "Beefsteak" (Seitan) recipe, but add a blend of canned smoked chipotle peppers in adobo sauce and Worcestershire sauce puréed in a food processor. Bear in mind that these peppers pack a punch, so not many are required. Simply sprinkle this puréed mixture over seitan during the sauté phase of preparation, along with some fresh lemon or lime juice, then serve on a toasted sandwich roll with melted white cheddar.

For Seared "Beef" and Vegetable Stir-Fry with Spicy Peanut Sauce

Follow Vegetarian "Beefsteak" (Seitan) recipe and boost the flavor with the **Grit's Spicy Sauce**. In a pinch, use a bottle of prepared peanut satay sauce from the natural food section at the supermarket. Prepare seitan as described and set aside. Prepare your favorite Asian noodles or rice and top with fresh vegetable and Grit Vegetarian "Beefsteak" sizzled together with a generous addition of spicy peanut sauce. When served at the Grit, this dish includes fresh spinach, mushrooms, carrots, broccoli, sugar snap peas, and water chestnuts.

One Great Seitan Entrée

Spinach Quesadilla

2 (10-ounce) packages frozen
    spinach, thawed
Butter or oil
1/2 small or 1/4 large yellow onion,
    finely minced
1 to 2 teaspoons minced fresh garlic
1/2 cup shredded carrots
1/2 to 2/3 cups fresh or frozen corn
1 teaspoon salt
1/4 teaspoon cumin powder
3/4 teaspoon chopped fresh
    coriander or 1/4 teaspoon dried
3/4 teaspoon chopped fresh oregano
    or 1/4 teaspoon dried

3/4 teaspoon chopped fresh basil or
    1/4 teaspoon dried
3/4 teaspoon chopped fresh parsley
    or 1/4 teaspoon dried
Large pinch cayenne pepper
Scant pinch freshly ground nutmeg
Butter or vegetable oil
4 large flour tortillas
4 cups shredded mild white cheddar
    cheese
1/2 cup **Grit Salsa**
1/4 cup sour cream

Thaw spinach and squeeze by hand to remove as much moisture as possible; set aside.

Lightly butter or oil bottom of a large saucepan. Sauté onion and garlic over medium-high heat until translucent, then add carrots, corn, herbs, and spices. Continue to sauté until vegetables are tender but still bright in color. Reduce heat to low and add spinach in loosened handfuls. Toss well with other ingredients and sauté just long enough to tenderize spinach.

Place a skillet lightly coated with butter or vegetable oil over medium-high heat and lay a tortilla inside. Cover with a handful of cheese and a layer of 1/4 of the spinach mixture. When cheese begins to melt, fold tortilla in half. Brown each side of quesadilla as desired and repeat with remaining tortillas. Serve with **Grit Salsa** and sour cream.

Yields 4 servings.

Cilantro Pesto and White Bean Quesadilla

Leaves of 12 cilantro stems
1/2 cup walnuts
1/2 cup freshly grated Parmesan cheese
1/4 teaspoon minced fresh garlic
1/4 teaspoon freshly ground black pepper
Extra-virgin olive oil
1 (15.5-ounce) can white beans, drained
Butter or vegetable oil
4 large flour tortillas
4 cups shredded mild white cheddar cheese
1/2 cup **Grit Salsa**
1/4 cup sour cream

In food processor, combine cilantro, walnuts, Parmesan cheese, garlic, and black pepper and pulse to combine. Slowly add just enough olive oil to make a thick pesto. Puree until smooth. In a medium mixing bowl, gently combine white beans and pesto.

Place a skillet lightly coated with butter or vegetable oil over medium-high heat and lay a tortilla inside. Cover with a handful of cheese and a layer of 1/4 of the pesto and white bean mixture. When cheese begins to melt, fold tortilla in half. Brown each side of quesadilla as desired. Repeat with remaining tortillas. Serve with **Grit Salsa** and sour cream.

Yields 4 servings.

Quesadillas, One Mondo Burrito, and a Casserole

Quesadillas,
One Mondo
Burrito, and a
Casserole

Roasted Corn and Zucchini Quesadilla

2 medium zucchinis, quartered lengthwise and sliced
2 cups frozen corn, frozen
1 teaspoon paprika
Olive oil
Leaves of 12 cilantro stems, minced
1/2 teaspoon salt
1/4 teaspoon freshly ground black pepper
Butter or vegetable oil
4 large flour tortillas
4 cups shredded mild white cheddar cheese
1/2 cup Grit Salsa
1/4 cup sour cream

Preheat oven to 400°F.

Combine zucchini and corn in a bowl. Gently toss with paprika and enough olive oil to lightly coat vegetables. Spread out evenly on a baking pan. Roast in the oven for 20 minutes or until zucchini and corn are slightly browned. Occasionally turn vegetables with a spatula during roasting. Remove from oven and gently stir together with cilantro, salt, and pepper; set aside.

Place a skillet lightly coated with butter or vegetable oil over medium-high heat and lay a tortilla inside. Cover with a handful of cheese and a layer of 1/4 of the zucchini and corn mixture. When cheese begins to melt, fold tortilla in half. Brown each side of quesadilla as desired and repeat with remaining tortillas. Serve with Grit Salsa and sour cream.

Yields 4 servings.

Red Bell Pepper and "Sausage" Quesadilla

Olive oil
8 vegetarian "sausage" links, finely chopped
3 medium or 2 large red bell peppers, sliced
2 medium yellow onions, sliced
Leaves of 8 cilantro stems, minced
Butter or vegetable oil
4 large flour tortillas
4 cups shredded mild white cheddar cheese
1/2 cup Grit Salsa
1/4 cup sour cream

Place a skillet lightly greased with olive oil over medium-high heat. Add "sausage" and sauté until slightly browned. Add bell peppers and onions and sauté until peppers are soft and onions caramelized. Stir in cilantro and remove from heat.

Place a skillet lightly coated with butter or vegetable oil over medium-high heat and lay a tortilla inside. Cover with a handful of cheese and a layer of 1/4 of the sauteed ingredients. Repeat with remaining tortillas. Serve with Grit Salsa and sour cream.

Yields 4 servings.

Quesadillas,
One Mondo
Burrito, and a
Casserole

Quesadillas,
One Mondo
Burrito, and a
Casserole

Mondo Burrito

A humongous, open-faced burrito starring **Grit Black Bean Chili**. It rarely gets consumed at one sitting, lamentably escalating the to-go container portion of The Grit budget.

    I large flour tortilla, warmed
    I cup cooked brown rice, warmed
    I-1/2 cups **Grit Black Bean Chili** warmed
    I small or 1/2 medium red onion, diced
    1/4 cup green bell pepper, diced
    1/2 carrot, shredded
    1/4 cup red cabbage, shredded
    1/4 cup shredded mild white cheddar cheese
    1/2 cup **Grit Salsa**

Lay tortilla on a large, oven-safe dinner plate and cover with rice and chili. Layer with vegetables and top with cheese.

Place under broiler in oven until cheese is melted and edge of tortilla is browned. Pour **Grit Salsa** onto tortilla to form a ring around edge of toppings.

Yields 1 to 2 servings.

Grit-Style Chilaquile Casserole

Another way to enjoy Grit Pintos or, in a pinch, canned seasoned pinto beans. Ideally, toss on some Grit Salsa just before serving.

2 tablespoons butter, divided	5 soft taco-size (8-inch) flour tortillas
1 small or 1/2 large yellow onion,	(white or whole wheat), divided
finely chopped	4 cups shredded white cheddar
1 large or 2 small garlic cloves, minced	cheese, divided
1 small zucchini, chopped	1 medium jalapeño pepper (or 2 if
(approximately 2 cups)	desired), minced
1 medium yellow squash, chopped	2 cups Grit Pintos or canned
(approximately 2 cups)	seasoned pinto beans
1/2 teaspoon cumin powder	3 eggs
1/2 teaspoon dried basil	1-1/2 cups buttermilk
1/2 teaspoon dried oregano	1/4 teaspoon dry or prepared
1 teaspoon salt	mustard

Preheat oven to 350°F. Grease a 9 x 13-inch pan or glass casserole dish with 1 tablespoon butter and set aside.

In a large skillet or frying pan, melt 1 tablespoon butter over high heat. Add onion and garlic, and sauté until onions are softened. Add zucchini, squash, dry spices, and salt. Tossing frequently for even cooking, sauté until vegetables are fully tender and onions are caramelized. Set aside.

Tear 3 tortillas by hand into random strips 2 to 3 inches wide. Distribute tortilla strips into bottoms of casserole dish, layering evenly (retain remaining 2 tortillas for top crust). Spread 2 cups of shredded cheese over torn tortillas. Sprinkle minced jalapeño evenly over cheese, followed by a layer of the pinto beans. Spread sautéed vegetables over this, and top evenly with remaining cheese. Tear remaining 2 tortillas as before and distribute on top to form upper crust. Beat eggs together with buttermilk and mustard. Pour mixture over casserole and place in oven. Bake for 35 to 40 minutes, until bubbling at the edges and well browned on top. Cool for 10 minutes before serving. Top with Grit Salsa.

Yields 8 servings.

Quesadillas, One Mondo Burrito, and a Casserole

sauces and gravies

From hearty and savory to sweet and tangy, the sauces and gravies at The Grit are extremely versatile. We invite you to use them as suggested or to strike out on your own and use them to enrich dishes we never dreamed of. But don't get too carried away—have some biscuits with that gravy!

- Lemon Dijon Butter
- Honey-Lime Glaze
- Tangerine-Maple Glaze
- Teriyaki Sauce
- Spicy Peanut Sauce
- Sage and Onion Gravy
- White "Sausage" Gravy
- Caramelized Onion and Red Wine Brown Sauce
- Butternut Squash Cream Sauce
- Grit Noodle Bowl Sauce #1: Citrus Szechuan
- Grit Noodle Bowl Sauce #2: Coconut-Ginger Curry

Sauces and
Gravies

Lemon Dijon Butter

Drizzle over steamed broccoli or vegetable of choice.

> 1/2 cup (1 stick) butter
> 3 tablespoons freshly squeezed lemon juice
> 2 tablespoons Dijon mustard
> 1 generous tablespoon chopped fresh parsley or 1-1/4 teaspoon dried
> 1/4 teaspoon salt
> 1/4 teaspoon freshly ground black pepper

Heat butter in saucepan over low heat or microwave just until melted. Place in food processor or blender and blend with all other ingredients until fully combined.

Yields 2/3 cup.

Honey-Lime Glaze

Wonderful drizzled over steamed baby carrots or fried plantains—peeled ripe plantains sliced into 1-inch-thick coins and fried in vegetable oil until very tender, then sprinkled lightly with salt.

> 1/2 cup (1 stick) butter
> 1/4 cup honey
> 2 tablespoons freshly squeezed lime juice
> Generous pinch of salt or dash of soy sauce

Heat butter in saucepan over low heat or microwave just until melted. Place in food processor or blender and blend with all other ingredients until fully combined

Yields 2/3 cup.

Tangerine-Maple Glaze

Served at The Grit over steamed baby carrots.

> 1/2 cup (1 stick) butter
> 3 tablespoons pure maple syrup
> 2 tablespoons tangerine juice concentrate
> Generous pinch of salt or dash of soy sauce

Heat butter in saucepan over low heat or microwave just until melted. Place in food processor or blender and blend with all other ingredients until fully combined.

Yields 2/3 cup.

Teriyaki Sauce Ⓥ

This delicious sauce can be whisked together by hand or in a blender. Enjoy it on stir-fried vegetables or our popular **Teriyaki Tofu Wrap Sandwich**.

> 3/4 cup rice wine vinegar
> 1 cup soy sauce
> 1 tablespoon pineapple or orange-pineapple juice concentrate
> 1-1/2 teaspoon chili sauce
> 1 teaspoon packed light brown sugar
> 3/4 teaspoon ginger powder

> 1/2 teaspoon Dijon mustard
> 1/8 teaspoon onion powder
> Pinch of granulated garlic
> Freshly squeezed juice of 1 large lemon
> 2 or 3 drops of chili oil (optional)

Combine all ingredients in a bowl or blender. Whisk or blend thoroughly, cover, and refrigerate. Make teriyaki sauce at least 2 hours in advance of use as flavors marry and taste improves.

Yields 2 cups.

Sauces and Gravies

Spicy Peanut Sauce

Great over steamed broccoli or stir-fried vegetables.

3/4 cup creamy peanut butter
1/2 cup freshly squeezed orange juice
1/4 cup cider vinegar
2 tablespoons soy sauce
2 tablespoons dark molasses
1/2 teaspoon cayenne pepper

Heat peanut butter and orange juice in a saucepan over medium heat and stir until well-blended and smooth. Add remaining ingredients, whisking frequently, and bring to a gentle boil for 1 to 2 minutes. Use immediately.

Yields 1-3/4 cups.

"The Grit—just the name makes me smile. The Grit is my favorite restaurant in America. I've spent weeks on tour in anticipation just counting down the days until we'd arrive in Athens, home of The Grit. I'd try to make sure that I'd have a day off to fill myself with good food to stave off the inevitable culinary letdown brought on by the rest of the country."

—PETER STUART, DOG'S EYE VIEW

Sage and Onion Gravy V

Vegan companion to our much-ballyhooed **Tofu "Meatloaf."**

2-2/3 cups water	1/2 teaspoon salt
1/4 cup soy sauce	1-1/2 teaspoon ground sage or
2 tablespoons vegan margarine	2 teaspoons rubbed sage
2 large yellow onions, thinly sliced	1/2 scant teaspoon white pepper
1/4 cup all-purpose flour	1 generous tablespoon onion powder
1/4 cup nutritional yeast	Pinch of dry mustard (optional)

Combine water and soy sauce; set aside.

    Melt margarine in a saucepan over medium-high heat and add sliced onions. Sauté until onions are translucent, approximately 3 minutes. Reduce heat to medium-low and add remaining ingredients. Cook for 5 minutes, stirring often. Increase heat enough to maintain simmer while gradually adding water and soy sauce mixture. Stir continuously over heat until gravy thickens, approximately 5 minutes.

Yields 4 cups.

Sauces and

Gravies

Sauces and Gravies

White "Sausage" Gravy

Please your carnivorous pals with this stuff. It's very rich and goes great on biscuits, eggs, brunch potatoes, et cetera!

1/2 cup (1 stick), plus 1 tablespoon butter

8 breakfast link vegetarian "sausages," such as Morningstar Farms, frozen

1/2 scant cup all-purpose flour

4 cups whole milk

2 tablespoons vegan Worcestershire sauce

1-1/2 teaspoon salt

1/2 teaspoon freshly ground black pepper

1/2 scant teaspoon ground sage

1/2 scant teaspoon dried rosemary

Melt 1 tablespoon butter in skillet and add frozen "sausages." Fry until thawed, remove from skillet, and chop into small pieces. Return "sausage" to skillet and fry until well done; set aside.

In a heavy-bottom saucepan, melt 1/2 cup butter, stir in flour, and heat just until mixture bubbles. Maintain bubbling, stirring well and almost constantly, for 4 minutes. Use no more heat than necessary. Gradually add milk, 1 cup at a time, while stirring vigorously. Allow mixture to thicken between additions. Add Worcestershire sauce and spices with the last addition. Adjust heat as necessary to thicken roux. Add prepared "sausage," stirring 2 minutes over heat until well blended. Remove from heat and allow to sit 5 to 10 minutes before serving. Milk may be added to thin the gravy.

Yields 4 cups.

Caramelized Onion and Red Wine Brown Sauce

Sauces and Gravies

This rich brown sauce boasts the flavors of caramelized red onions and a varied array of libations, offering a distinct and complex taste ideal for **Tofu Wellington** or **Herbed Dumplings**.

6 tablespoons (3/4 stick) margarine or butter	3 tablespoons brown sugar
1 large or 2 small red onions, finely minced	1 teaspoon salt
	1 teaspoon black pepper
1 cup red wine	1 teaspoon dried thyme
1/4 cup soy sauce	1 teaspoon dried parsley
2 tablespoons molasses	1 tablespoon cornstarch
3 tablespoons minced garlic	3 cups water
	3 tablespoons brandy

Melt margarine or butter in a large saucepan or stockpot. Add onions and cook over medium-high heat, stirring frequently to avoid burning, until onions are nearly lique-fied and deeply browned.

Continue to stir frequently during the addition of ingredients. Add red wine, soy sauce, and molasses and cook for 2 minutes. Blend in minced garlic, brown sugar, salt, pepper, and dried spices and cook for 2 minutes. Blend cornstarch into water and add to the sauce. Stir in brandy and continue to cook over medium-high heat, stirring often, until the sauce thickens (approximately 5 minutes).

Yields 4 cups.

Sauces and
Gravies

Butternut Squash Cream Sauce

This decadent sauce combines the sweetly robust flavor of roasted butternut squash with the richness of butter and heavy cream. It's perfect over **Herbed Dumplings** or served with **Tofu Wellington** for a taste of Grit specials at their most extraordinary.

1/4 cup white flour
3 tablespoons minced fresh parsley
    or 1 teaspoon dried parsley
1 tablespoon Parmesan cheese
2 teaspoons salt
2 teaspoons sugar
1 teaspoon thyme
1/2 teaspoon black pepper
1/2 teaspoon ground rosemary
1 dash cinnamon

1 dash cayenne pepper
1 dash rubbed sage
1 medium butternut squash
1 can (14-ounce) coconut milk
1/2 cup (1 stick) butter
1 medium yellow onion, finely
    chopped
1-1/2 teaspoon minced garlic
1 cup milk
1 cup heavy cream

Preheat oven to 400°F.

Combine the first 11 ingredients (all dry ingredients including Parmesan cheese) thoroughly and set aside.

Cut the butternut squash in half lengthwise and remove the seeds and pulp with a spoon. Place squash skin side up on a baking sheet pan with just enough water on the pan to cover the bottom. Roast squash for 45 minutes or until it is soft to the touch and easily pierced by a utensil. When squash has cooled, use a spoon to scoop flesh from squash and place flesh in a blender or food processor with coconut milk. Purée until very smooth and creamy. Set aside.

Melt butter in a saucepan over medium heat and add onion and garlic. Sauté until onion is soft and translucent. Gradually stir in the combined dry ingredients to form a thick paste. Using just enough heat to maintain a slight but steady bubbling, stir almost constantly for approximately 6 minutes. Slowly stir in milk and heavy cream, and stir constantly over medium-low heat until sauce begins to thicken.

Stir in the squash and coconut milk mixture, and whisk thoroughly until well blended with sauce. Continue to whisk often, cooking over medium-low heat for 15 to 20 minutes or just until very hot.

Yields approximately 4 cups.

Noodle Bowls of the Grit

Providing gargantuan servings of saucy, steaming noodles with bright veggies and spicy, chunky tofu has been a paramount public service and perennial pleasure for our pantry to perform. Please do try these at home.

Grit Noodle Bowl Sauce #1: Citrus Szechuan Ⓥ

2-1/2 cups orange juice (preferably
    squeezed fresh)
1 cup pineapple juice
3/4 cup soy sauce
1/4 cup brown sugar
3 tablespoons squeezed lemon juice
2 tablespoons hot chili sauce (we use
    Sriracha brand)

2 tablespoons molasses
2 tablespoons rice wine vinegar
1-1/2 teaspoon ginger powder
3 tablespoons cornstarch
1/2 cup water

In a 2-quart saucepan, combine all ingredients except cornstarch and water. Place over medium-high heat and stir occasionally until mixture begins to simmer. Blend cornstarch into water and add to sauce. Bring mixture to a full boil, stirring often, for at least 1 minute or until thickened. Remove from heat. The yield is 4 1-cup servings.

This sauce is usually served at The Grit over pressed, sautéed, and seasoned tofu (or sautéed, seasoned tempeh), sautéed red bell peppers, onions, and green beans or sugar snap peas and with thick canton noodles (but will be enjoyable over vegetables, noodles, and protein of your choice).

Sauces and Gravies

"The bowl is deep, the noodles wide.
Among them many flavors hide.
The Grit's been gettin' Asian food on.
Open wide and bring the Udon!"

Sauces and Gravies

Grit Noodle Bowl Sauce #2: Coconut-Ginger Curry ⓥ

3 tablespoons olive oil
3 tablespoons finely minced fresh
ginger
2 tablespoons finely minced garlic
2 (14-ounce) cans coconut milk
1/2 cup shredded coconut
(sweetened or unsweetened as
desired)
1/4 cup soy sauce
1/4 cup apricot preserves

1 teaspoon hot chili sauce (we use
Sriracha brand)
3/4 teaspoon salt
1/2 teaspoon ginger powder
1/4 teaspoon turmeric
1/4 teaspoon coriander
1/4 teaspoon cayenne pepper
4 teaspoons cornstarch
1/2 cup water

In a 2-quart saucepan, heat olive oil over medium-high heat and add minced fresh ginger and garlic. Sauté until slightly browned, then add all other ingredients except cornstarch and water. Bring mixture to a gentle boil.

Blend cornstarch into water and add to sauce. Stir frequently, bringing mixture to a full boil for at least 1 minute or until slightly thickened. Remove from heat. The yield is four 1-cup servings.

This sauce is usually served at The Grit over pressed, sautéed, and seasoned tofu (or sautéed, seasoned tempeh), sautéed broccoli, carrots, and mushrooms and with udon noodles (but will be enjoyable over vegetables, noodles, and protein of your choice).

vegetables
and side dishes

Folks want our daily veggie selections posted on the Internet but we have a hard enough time keeping our two chalk-board menus up to date. So here's something better than knowing what the vegetables of the day are—knowing how to make them yourself.

Vegetables and
Side Dishes

Grit Guacamole

Guac is a great way to start any meal, even the first of the day. The Grit's guac has a secret weapon: Grit Salsa. Not only does the salsa boost the flavor of the guacamole, but they're also great companions, served side by side with chips. So whip up some salsa! Otherwise, compensate by substituting hot sauce and a touch more vinegar or citrus.

    4-1/2 cups mashed ripe avocado (approximately 8 medium avocados)
    1/3 cup sour cream
    Freshly squeezed juice of 1/2 lemon or 1 lime
    2 tablespoons Grit Salsa
    1 cup chopped ripe tomatoes, slightly drained
    1/3 cup very finely minced red onion
    1 teaspoon salt
    1/4 teaspoon freshly ground black pepper
    1/8 teaspoon granulated garlic

After peeling, coring, and mashing avocados to desired consistency (we prefer slightly chunky) combine with all ingredients and stir until fully combined. Cover and refrigerate. Serve well chilled.

Yields 5 cups or about 10 servings.

Vegans can substitute 1/2 (12.3-ounce) package silken tofu for sour cream.

Baby Lima Beans

3 pounds fresh baby lima beans, shelled, or 1 pound frozen
Water
1 to 2 tablespoons butter
1 small or 1/2 large yellow onion, finely chopped
2 tablespoons vegan Worcestershire sauce
1 generous teaspoon salt
1/4 teaspoon white pepper
1 tablespoon Grit Yeast Gravy (optional)

Place lima beans in a pot with just enough water to cover, then add 1 cup water. Place over high heat and bring to a boil while onions are being prepared.

In a sauté pan, melt butter and add onion. Cook over high heat, stirring well, until onions are caramelized, approximately 5 minutes. Add onions to limas, scraping every bit of browned onion and butter into pot. Add all other ingredients to limas and boil, stirring often, until beans reach desired tenderness. If necessary, add water in small increments to maintain proper boiling.

Yields 4 to 5 servings.

"I like to get vegetables from the specials board and color coordinate them. It doesn't matter which dish, they are always delicious. I also go to The Grit not only for the vitamins but because I always run into somebody I'm glad to see—customer or employee."

—ARMISTEAD WELLFORD, LOVE TRACTOR

Vegetables and
Side Dishes

Vegetables and Side Dishes

Collard Greens

collard \kä-l\rd\ n. [alter. of colewort, 1755]: A kind of kale (*Brassica oleracea acephala*) whose coarse leaves are borne in tufts.

The secret ingredient is the **Grit Yeast Gravy,** y'all.

> 1 large bunch (about 3 pounds) fresh collard greens, well rinsed
> Water
> 3/4 cup **Grit Yeast Gravy**
> 1/2 cup cider vinegar
> 2 tablespoons soy sauce
> 1 tablespoon sugar
> 2 teaspoons hot sauce
> 1 teaspoon dry mustard
> 1-3/4 teaspoon salt
> 1/2 teaspoon white pepper
> 1/4 teaspoon baking soda

Strip stems from leaves of collards. Roll handfuls of leaves as if rolling a cigar and chiffonade into narrow strips, then chop strips into smaller pieces. Place in a large stockpot. Add enough water to cover greens when greens are forced down by hand into bottom of pot, then add 3 cups water.

Place pot over high heat, stir in remaining ingredients, and cover. Bring to a vigorous boil, stirring occasionally, and cook greens 35 minutes to 1 hour, depending on desired tenderness. Check flavor and adjust seasonings as desired.

Yields 8 to 10 servings.

Creamed Spinach

A light, tangy version made with plain yogurt. Frozen spinach should be loose—frozen in a bag, not in a block.

- 1 tablespoon plus 1 teaspoon butter
- 1/2 medium yellow onion, finely minced
- 2 pounds fresh crinkly leaf spinach, well rinsed and stems trimmed,
  or 1 pound frozen
- 1 cup plain yogurt
- 1/4 teaspoon Dijon or coarse-grained mustard
- Generous pinch of freshly ground black pepper
- Very small pinch of freshly ground nutmeg
- 2 teaspoons vegan Worcestershire sauce

Melt butter in a medium saucepan and add onion. Sauté over medium-high heat until caramelized, approximately 5 minutes. Add spinach and cover, stirring frequently over medium-high heat until fully softened and thoroughly warmed through.

Stir in yogurt and spices. Add Worcestershire sauce and continue cooking and stirring over medium heat until spinach is satisfactorily tender.

Yields 2 to 3 servings.

Vegetables and Side Dishes

Vegetables and Side Dishes

Green Beans with White Wine and Mustard Sauce

A fast and flavorful vegetable side for two. Whip it up just before serving the main course.

> 2 tablespoons olive oil
> 1 teaspoon butter
> 1/2 to 2/3 pound green beans, tipped and trimmed
> 1/4 cup dry white wine
> 2 teaspoons pure maple syrup
> 1/4 teaspoon cider vinegar
> 1/2 teaspoon Dijon or horseradish mustard
> 1/8 teaspoon salt or generous dash of soy sauce

Place olive oil and butter in 10-inch skillet over high heat. When butter is melted, add green beans and sauté, covered but stirring often, until bright green and softened slightly.

Add white wine and cover, simmering for 30 to 40 seconds. Add remaining ingredients and continue cooking on high heat and tossing until sauce begins to thicken. Beans should be dark green and tender but still slightly firm to the bite. Serve immediately.

Yields 2 servings.

Green Bean Casserole

3 pounds frozen green beans
Hot water
4 tablespoons butter, divided
1 medium yellow onion, finely chopped
2-1/2 cups fine breadcrumbs, divided
2 large eggs, beaten
4 cups shredded mild cheddar cheese
2 (10.75-ounce) cans cream of celery soup
1 tablespoon vegan Worcestershire sauce
1 teaspoon salt
1/2 teaspoon freshly ground black pepper

Preheat oven to 350°F. Grease a 9 x 13-inch pan or glass casserole.

Thaw frozen green beans completely in hot water. Drain thoroughly; set aside.

Melt 2 tablespoons butter in a sauté pan and add onion. Sauté over high heat until very soft and translucent, approximately 5 minutes. Combine green beans, onion, 1/2 cup breadcrumbs, and all other ingredients in a large bowl and stir together until fully combined. Transfer to prepared pan and spread evenly.

Melt remaining butter, mix with breadcrumbs and spread topping over casserole. Bake for 1 hour or until green beans in center of casserole are extremely tender and topping is very well browned.

Yields 10 to 12 servings.

Vegetables and
Side Dishes

Vegetables and Side Dishes

Squash Casserole

4 pounds frozen cut yellow squash
Hot water
4 tablespoons butter, divided
1 small onion, finely chopped
2-1/2 cups fine breadcrumbs, divided
2 large eggs, beaten
4 cups shredded sharp cheddar cheese
1 (10.75-ounce) can cream of celery soup
1 teaspoon salt
1/4 teaspoon freshly ground black pepper

Preheat oven to 350°F. Grease a 9 x 13-inch pan or glass casserole.

Thaw frozen squash completely in hot water. Drain and gently press out as much water as possible; set aside.

Melt 2 tablespoons butter in a sauté pan and add onion. Sauté over high heat until very soft and translucent, approximately 3 to 5 minutes. Combine squash, onion, 1/2 cup breadcrumbs, and all other ingredients in a large bowl and stir together until fully combined, doing so gently enough to retain the body of the tender squash slices. Transfer to prepared pan and spread evenly.

Melt remaining butter, mix with breadcrumbs, and spread topping over casserole. Bake for 1 hour or until squash in center of casserole is extremely tender and topping is very well browned.

Yields 10 to 12 servings.

For broccoli casserole, substitute 7 cups of chopped broccoli that has been steamed or boiled until tender but not soft, about 5 minutes.

Mac and Cheese

Creamy in the middle, crispy on the top. Try to eat a little, but honk down 'til you pop!

    4 cups (1 pound) dried elbow macaroni
    12 cups water
    6 tablespoons butter, divided
    2 large eggs, slightly beaten
    4 cups whole milk
    1 generous teaspoon mustard, dry or prepared
    2 teaspoons salt
    Pinch of black or cayenne pepper
    1 tablespoon plus 1 teaspoon hot sauce
    6 cups shredded sharp cheddar cheese
    1-1/2 cups fine breadcrumbs

Preheat oven to 425°F. Grease a 9 x 13-inch pan or glass casserole.

Bring water to a rolling boil in a large stockpot. Add macaroni and boil 8 to 10 minutes or just until al dente. Remove and drain well; set aside.

Melt 3 tablespoons butter in the stockpot and add drained pasta, stirring to combine. Whisk together eggs, milk, mustard, salt, pepper, and hot sauce. Add to pasta and cheese. Stir mixture constantly over medium-high heat until cheese melts and milk and eggs begin to thicken. Continue cooking, stirring constantly, for 5 minutes or until very thick and creamy. Transfer to prepared casserole.

Melt remaining butter in a small saucepan and mix with breadcrumbs. Spread mixture evenly over top of macaroni mixture. Bake 10 to 15 minutes. May be further browned by briefly placing under broiler, if desired.

Yields 10 to 12 servings.

Vegetables and Side Dishes

"We're always trying to figure out in our kitchen at home what makes this Grit dish or that one *soooo* killer. Now we don't have to wonder. It is my favorite restaurant in North America (because in Europe, there's Italy)."

—VIC CHESNUTT

Vegetables and Side Dishes

Sweet Potato Casserole

Choose sweet potatoes with bright orange flesh.

4 pounds (4 jumbo) sweet potatoes, peeled and sliced
Water
1 large egg, beaten
3 cups grated mild cheddar cheese
1 teaspoon salt
1/2 teaspoon white pepper
1/2 teaspoon freshly ground cinnamon
Pinch of freshly ground nutmeg
Very small pinch of freshly ground cloves
2/3 cup melted butter
2/3 cup all-purpose flour
1-1/4 cup chopped walnuts
3/4 cup packed light brown sugar

Preheat oven to 375°F. Grease a 9 x 13-inch pan or glass casserole.

Place sweet potatoes in a large pot and add enough cold water to cover by 1 inch. Bring to a boil and cook 10 to 12 minutes, or until tender when pierced with a knife tip or thin skewer. Drain well and transfer to a large mixing bowl. Add egg, cheese, salt, pepper, cinnamon, nutmeg, and cloves. Mash together and stir vigorously until well blended. Transfer to prepared pan. Thoroughly combine butter, flour, walnuts, and brown sugar in a small mixing bowl. Spread over top of sweet potato mixture. Bake 35 to 40 minutes or until top is well browned and casserole has become slightly firmed.

Yields 8 to 10 servings.

Whipped Sweet Potatoes

4 pounds (4 jumbo) sweet potatoes
2 tablespoons butter or vegan margarine
1 teaspoon salt
1/2 teaspoon packed light brown sugar
1/8 teaspoon white pepper

Preheat oven to 425°F.

  Pierce sweet potatoes several times with a paring knife. Place on a foil-lined cookie sheet in oven and roast at least 45 minutes, or until they are completely soft, beginning to caramelize, and a knife glides through them with ease. Remove from oven and cool exterior of potatoes slightly by immersing in cool water. Remove peels and place potatoes in a medium mixing bowl. Add other ingredients and stir, then whip together with electric mixer on high speed. Blend until creamy and smooth. Serve immediately.

Yields 6 to 8 servings.

If sweet potatoes are extremely large, roasting can be hastened by roasting them with an all-metal knife inserted into the center of each potato, to draw heat within.

For tropical sweet potatoes, add any or all of the following: 1 to 2 tablespoons freshly squeezed lime juice, 1 generous tablespoon pineapple or orange-pineapple juice concentrate, 1/2 cup coconut milk.

Vegetables and
Side Dishes

Vegetables and Side Dishes

Garlic-Parsley Mashed Potatoes

If this dairy-laden deluxe delight isn't on the menu board, please notify management—something is amiss at The Grit!

4 pounds boiling potatoes, such as round white, round red, or Yukon Gold
Water
Salt
2 tablespoons butter
1 small or 1/2 large yellow onion, finely chopped
1 tablespoon minced fresh garlic
2-1/2 teaspoons salt
1/2 teaspoon white pepper
Generous pinch of freshly ground black pepper
1/2 teaspoon granulated garlic
3/4 cup sour cream
1/2 cup whole milk
1 bunch fresh parsley, minced, or 3 tablespoons dried parsley

Scrub and partially peel potatoes. Place in a large pot and add enough cold water to cover by 1 inch. Add 1 teaspoon salt for each quart of water used. Bring to a boil over high heat and cook 10 to 15 minutes, or until tender when pierced with a knife tip or thin skewer.

While potatoes boil, melt butter in a large skillet and add onion and fresh garlic. Sauté briefly and add salt, white pepper, black pepper, and granulated garlic. Continue to sauté over medium-high heat, stirring frequently, until onions are well browned.

Drain cooked potatoes well and combine all ingredients in a large mixing bowl or stockpot. Mash vigorously by hand or use electric mixer to blend to creamy smoothness.

Yields 8 servings.

Spanish Rice

A great use for leftover Grit Salsa and Grit Marinara.

3 cloves fresh garlic
I large onion
I tablespoon olive oil
I small or I/2 large green bell pepper, finely minced
2 ripe medium tomatoes, or 4 ripe Roma or plum tomatoes, finely minced
4 cups steamed rice
Freshly squeezed juice of I large lemon
I cup Grit Salsa
I/4 cup Grit Marinara
I teaspoon green jalapeño hot sauce or other hot sauce
2 teaspoons salt
Pinch of freshly ground black pepper
Pinch of cumin powder

In a large food processor, puree I clove garlic and I/2 of onion. Finely mince remaining onion and garlic.

Heat olive oil in a large pan and add green pepper, tomatoes, and remaining garlic and onions. Cook over high heat, stirring well, for a few minutes until garlic and onion are thoroughly cooked. Reduce heat to medium and stir in cooked rice, then remaining ingredients. Cook until very hot, but remove from heat before rice becomes mushy.

Yield 6 servings.

Vegetables and
Side Dishes

Vegetables and Side Dishes

Creamed Corn

5 large ears corn, cooked and kernels cut from cob (about 4 cups) or
   2 (16-ounce) bags frozen white baby corn, thawed
Vegetable oil
1-1/4 teaspoon salt
1/2 teaspoon freshly ground black pepper
1-1/2 cups hot water
2 teaspoons cornstarch

Combine hot water and cornstarch; set aside.

Place 1 cup of corn in a food processor and puree. Add remaining corn and process until coarsely ground.

Lightly oil the bottom of a large, heavy saucepan, add all corn and place over gentle heat. Stir in salt, pepper, and cornstarch mixture. Bring corn mixture to a gentle, bubbling simmer, stirring often. Maintain gentle simmer and stir frequently until mixture thickens and has a delicious roasted corn aroma.

Yields 4 servings.

Okra, Corn, and Tomatoes

Always tangy, saucy, and available at The Grit.

- 1 tablespoon butter
- 1 medium yellow onion, finely chopped
- 2 ripe medium tomatoes or 4 ripe Roma or plum tomatoes
- 1 (28-ounce) can diced tomatoes
- 2-1/2 to 3 cups fresh or frozen okra, cut into 1/3-inch coins
- 2 cups fresh cooked or frozen corn, thawed
- 1 tablespoon plus 1 teaspoon cider vinegar
- 1 tablespoon vegan Worcestershire sauce
- 2 teaspoons dry mustard
- 1-1/2 teaspoon salt
- 1/4 teaspoon white pepper
- Generous pinch of filé powder
- 8 cups steamed rice

Melt butter in a large pot and add onion. Cook over high heat until sizzling, then add fresh tomato. Cook briefly until tomatoes soften, stirring well. Add canned tomatoes and okra and continue cooking, stirring often, until okra is softened. Cover pot between stirrings to speed cooking.

Add all other ingredients and cook for 15 to 20 minutes over medium heat, stirring frequently, until corn and okra are tender to the bite. Serve over steamed rice.

Yields 8 servings.

Vegetables and
Side Dishes

Vegetables and
Side Dishes

Maple BBQ Baked Beans

They're intense. They're sweet. They're spicy. Okay, so they're not baked. Take them off the stove and stick 'em in your oven if you're gonna be a stickler about it!

3 (15.5-ounce) cans white navy beans
1/2 cup pure maple syrup
1/4 cup soy sauce
1/4 cup vegan Worcestershire sauce
1/4 cup ketchup
2 tablespoons cider vinegar
1 teaspoon salt
1 teaspoon dry mustard
1/4 scant teaspoon cayenne pepper
1/8 teaspoon ginger powder
Pinch of fresh chopped or dried thyme
Small pinch of freshly ground nutmeg

Combine all ingredients in a medium saucepan, heat to a gently bubbling simmer, and cook 5 to 8 minutes. Remove from heat and allow to sit 15 minutes so flavors can combine, then serve.

Yields 4 servings.

3 (15-ounce) blocks firm tofu
1 cup double-strength brewed coffee
1/2 cup cider vinegar
1/2 cup soy sauce
1 (14-ounce) bottle ketchup
1 tablespoon plus 1 teaspoon dark chili powder
1 tablespoon granulated garlic
1 tablespoon plus 1 teaspoon dry mustard
2-1/2 packed tablespoons light brown sugar
1/4 teaspoon cayenne pepper
6 to 8 cups steamed brown rice

Preheat oven to 350°F. Grease a large baking sheet.

Chop 1 block of tofu into cubes the size of dice. Shred remaining blocks of tofu by hand into an array of different-sized chunks until they resemble scrambled eggs. Spread all tofu on prepared baking sheet. Bake, tossing and turning frequently with a spatula until tofu becomes very firm and has a barely crispy exterior and a chewy, tender interior. Remove from oven.

As tofu bakes, combine all other ingredients in a saucepan. Stirring frequently, simmer until mixture begins to thicken. Combine with cooked tofu, stir well. Serve over steamed brown rice.

Yields 6 to 8 servings.

"When on tour, we usually don't get up until we've already ridden out of town. Hence we never eat until the next town. Unless we're in Athens. Then we set our alarms and get our asses out of bed. Or just stay up all night. All because of The Grit. We're all about The Grit."

—MARC PERLMAN, JAYHAWKS

Vegetables and Side Dishes

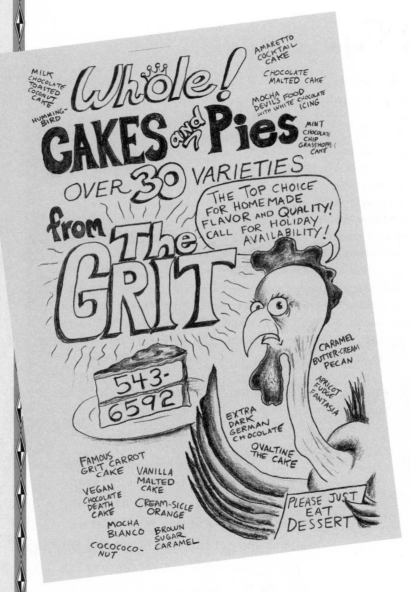

desserts

Few things are as disappointing as a dessert that looks better than it tastes, but that is what you find in many places. Granted, the first bite might be with the eye, but redemption occurs in the mouth. That's a fancy way of saying that at The Grit we believe that simple is best, fussy recipes stink, and our desserts are all the better for what's not thrown in. Less really *is* more in the case of spices in pies or flavor extracts in icings or cookies—nothing should get in the way of real fruit flavor or the power of chocolate. Here are some recipes that rock our world, from traditional takes to wacky originals. Bake away!

Chocolate-Chocolate Chip Cookies

1/2 cup (1 stick) butter, melted
3/4 cup plus 2 tablespoons sugar
1 large egg, at room temperature
1 teaspoon pure vanilla extract
3/4 cup plus 2 tablespoons all-purpose flour
1/3 cup plus 1 teaspoon cocoa powder
1/2 teaspoon baking soda
1/4 teaspoon salt
2/3 cup semisweet chocolate chips

Preheat oven to 375°F. Grease two 17 x 14-inch metal cookie sheets.

In a large mixing bowl, thoroughly cream together butter and sugar. Add egg and vanilla extract and beat until fully combined. In a medium mixing bowl, whisk together remaining ingredients except chocolate chips and add to butter mixture. Stir until well combined. Fold in chocolate chips until fully and evenly mixed into dough.

Scoop rounded tablespoons of dough onto prepared cookie sheets, flatten slightly with the palm of your hand or the bottom of a water glass.

Bake 10 minutes or until very lightly browned and center of cookies spring back from gentle pressure.

Yields 2 dozen cookies.

For Almond Mocha Chip Cookies, combine just enough pure vanilla extract to dissolve 1 generous tablespoon instant coffee powder and add mixture to dough, along with 1/2 cup sliced or slivered almonds, when mixing in chocolate chips.

Peanut Butter Chocolate Chip Cookies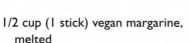

1/2 cup (1 stick) vegan margarine, melted

1/2 cup lightly packed light brown sugar

1/2 cup sugar

1/2 teaspoon pure vanilla extract

1 tablespoon water

1-1/2 teaspoon cornstarch

1-1/2 cups plus 2 tablespoons all-purpose flour, unsifted

3/4 teaspoon baking soda

1/2 teaspoon salt

3 tablespoons double-strength brewed coffee

6 tablespoons peanut butter

2/3 cup semisweet chocolate chips

Preheat oven to 375°F. Grease two 17 x 14-inch metal cookie sheets.

In a large mixing bowl with electric mixer on medium speed, cream margarine and sugars until fully blended. Add vanilla extract. Blend water and cornstarch, add to mixture and stir until fully combined. Sift together flour, baking soda, and salt. Add to margarine mixture and stir until fully combined. Add coffee and peanut butter. Stir just until combined. Fold in chocolate chips until fully and evenly mixed into dough. Scoop rounded tablespoons of dough onto greased sheet pan, flatten slightly with the palm of your hand or the bottom of a water glass.

Bake 10 minutes or until very lightly browned and centers of cookies spring back after gentle pressure.

Yields 2 dozen cookies.

Cookies and Brownies

Cookies and Brownies

Coconut-Orange Sugar Cookies

1/2 cup vegetable shortening, at room temperature

1 cup sugar, plus additional for topping the cookies

2 large eggs, at room temperature

2 tablespoons orange juice concentrate

1 tablespoon whole milk

1 teaspoon pure vanilla extract

2-1/2 cups all-purpose flour

1/4 teaspoon baking soda

1/2 teaspoon salt

1 cup sweetened flaked coconut

In a large mixing bowl with electric mixer on medium speed, cream together shortening, sugar, and eggs until fully blended. Stir in orange juice concentrate, milk, and vanilla extract. Whisk together flour, baking soda, and salt. Add to shortening mixture with coconut and stir until fully combined. Refrigerate 1 hour.

Preheat oven to 400°F. Grease three 11 x 17-inch cookie sheets.

Scoop rounded tablespoons of dough onto prepared cookie sheets, then flatten slightly with the palm of your hand or the bottom of a water glass dipped in sugar. Sprinkle generously with sugar.

Bake 8 to 10 minutes or until bottoms of cookies are gently browned.

Yields 3 dozen cookies.

"The Grit? I just came from there. I get my sweet on at The Grit!"

—DEXTER WEAVER,
Automatic Y'all:
Weaver D's Guide to the Soul

Put pleasure before polish. Sophisticated is nice, but home-style will do just fine.

1 cup (2 sticks) butter, melted	2 teaspoons double-acting baking
2 cups lightly packed light brown	powder
sugar	1/2 teaspoon salt
2 large eggs, at room temperature	1 cup semisweet chocolate chips
2 cups sifted all-purpose flour	1 cup walnut pieces

Preheat oven at 350°F. Grease a 9 x 13-inch metal baking pan.

In a large mixing bowl, combine butter and brown sugar. Stir until fully blended and cool. Add eggs separately, beating well after each addition. In a medium mixing bowl, whisk together flour, baking powder, and salt. Add to butter mixture and stir until fully combined. Fold in chocolate chips and walnuts pieces just until evenly blended into mixture. Pour batter into prepared pan.

Bake 35 minutes or until golden brown and slightly puffed up in center. Remove from oven and cool completely on a wire rack before cutting. Blondies will fall very slightly as they cool.

Yields 12 blondies.

"We've eaten at The Grit every time we've passed through Athens, every time enjoying the food and the hang, always made to feel right at home. Bring on the vegan desserts and bring back the poetry dances!"
—IAN MACKAYE, FUGAZI

Cookies and

Brownies

Cookies and
Brownies

Royal Canadian Cream Cheese Brownies

Brownies:

2 cups sugar

1 cup cocoa powder

1 cup (2 sticks) butter, melted

4 large eggs, at room temperature

2 teaspoons pure vanilla extract

1-1/3 cup all-purpose flour

1 teaspoon double-acting baking powder

1/2 teaspoon salt

Cream Cheese Topping:

2 (8-ounce) packages cream cheese, softened

2/3 cup sugar

2 large eggs, beaten

1 teaspoon pure vanilla extract

To prepare brownies: Preheat oven to 350°F. Grease a 9 x 13-inch baking pan.

In a large mixing bowl, whisk together sugar and cocoa powder. Using an electric mixer on medium speed, add butter and thoroughly cream together. Add eggs 1 at a time, mixing well after each addition. Blend in vanilla. In a small mixing bowl, whisk together flour, baking soda, and salt. Add to butter mixture and mix until fully combined. Pour into prepared pan; set aside.

To prepare cream cheese topping: Using an electric mixer on medium speed, beat cream cheese until smooth. Add sugar and thoroughly cream together. Beat in eggs and vanilla and thoroughly combine.

Pour onto brownie mixture and spread evenly to cover.

Bake 40 to 45 minutes or until a knife or toothpick inserted into center comes out clean. Remove from oven, and cool completely on a wire rack before cutting.

Yields 12 brownies.

Basic Pie Crust

1 cup all-purpose flour
Pinch of salt
Pinch of freshly ground cinnamon
  (optional)

1/3 cup plus 2 teaspoons vegetable
  shortening, chilled
1 cup ice water
1 tablespoon cider vinegar

Whisk together flour, salt, and cinnamon. Cut shortening into flour mixture with pastry blender until particles of shortening range in size from that of a chocolate chip to 1/2 the size of a chocolate chip. Blend ice water and cider vinegar and sprinkle evenly on dough 1 teaspoon at a time, lightly tossing with pastry blender after each addition. Continue just until dough is moist enough to form a cohesive ball. Test small portions by squeezing between fingers as liquid is added. While 5 or 6 teaspoons of liquid is usually sufficient, it is imperative that dough is tested as it is being made, since the condition of the flour or the humidity of the room can affect results. Use as little liquid as necessary.

With floured hands, form dough into ball and flatten ball into disc. Lay disc on lightly floured sheet of wax paper slightly larger than a 9-inch pie dish. Sprinkle dough lightly with flour and use floured bottom of pie dish to press dough into a flatter, wider symmetrical disc. Using a floured rolling pin and working from the center out in all directions, roll dough out thinly and evenly into a 13-inch round. Maintain circular shape and add minimal flour as needed.

Use layer of wax paper to flip dough over into pie dish. Center and gently press dough down into dish. Trim the edges with kitchen shears or knife, leaving a 3/4-inch overhang. Tuck the overhang under itself, resting the edge on the flared edge of the pie dish. Crimp the edges by pressing lightly with the tines of a fork, or flute the edges by pressing your thumb and index finger, held about 1 inch apart, against the outside of the rim, then poking an indentation through the space from the inside edge of the pie crust with the index finger of your other hand.

Crust can be prebaked or frozen for later use.

To prebake crust, line inside of crust with aluminum foil and fill with dry beans, rice, or metal pie weights. Bake in a preheated 350°F oven for 30 to 40 minutes or until golden brown on edges. (Beans and rice can be retained for the same use at later time.)

Yields 1 (9-inch) single-crust pie crust.

Double Pie Crust

The **Basic Pie Crust** recipe can be doubled for a double-crust pie. To form 2 crusts, divide dough in half and roll out crusts individually as described above, except that top crust should be only a 12-inch round. Line pie dish with bottom crust and form down into dish. Trim edges with a knife or kitchen shears, leaving a 3/4-inch overhang. Place pie filling in bottom crust and lay top crust over pie. Center top crust and press crusts together gently against rim of dish. Work around pie, rolling edges together and inward tightly toward center of pie to form a 3/8- to 1/2-inch ring of folded dough at edge. Crimp or flute edges of crust. Prick top with a fork or make small slashes with a knife to allow steam to vent.

An interesting twist on this basic dough is to use very finely ground graham cracker crumbs instead of flour when flattening and rolling out dough. This lends a heightened sweetness and pleasing texture to the crust and works well with any of our pie recipes.

Grade-A Classic Blueberry Pie

2 batches **Basic Pie Crust**, divided
2 tablespoons cornstarch
Freshly squeezed juice of 1/2 lemon
2 teaspoons pure vanilla extract
2 teaspoons brandy
4-1/2 cups fresh or frozen blueberries
1 cup sugar
2 tablespoons butter, chopped into small pieces
1 generous tablespoon sour cream
1 tablespoon flour
1/4 scant teaspoon freshly ground cinnamon

Preheat oven to 450°F. Line a deep-dish pie pan with 1 batch of **Basic Pie Crust**. Reserve second batch for top crust.

In a small mixing bowl, thoroughly blend cornstarch, lemon juice, vanilla extract, and brandy into a paste. Combine paste and remaining ingredients in a large bowl and gently stir together just until combined, using care not to damage berries. Transfer into pie crust and cover with top crust. Place pie on a large cookie sheet.

Bake at 450°F for 10 to 15 minutes, then reduce heat to 350°F. Bake an additional 45 to 55 minutes until golden brown and juice bubbles from top crust. Cool completely before serving.

Yields 8 to 10 servings.

Sour Cream Apple Pie

2 batches **Basic Pie Crust**, divided
2 tablespoons cornstarch
Freshly squeezed juice of 1/2 lemon
2 teaspoons pure vanilla extract
2 teaspoons brandy
4 large Granny Smith apples (or enough to yield 4-1/2 cups), peeled and cut
    into 1/4-inch slices
1-1/4 cups sugar
3 tablespoons sour cream
2 tablespoons butter, chopped into small pieces
1 tablespoon all-purpose flour
1/4 teaspoon freshly ground cinnamon

Preheat oven to 450°F. Line a pie pan with 1 batch of **Basic Pie Crust**

In a small mixing bowl, thoroughly blend cornstarch, lemon juice, vanilla extract, and brandy into a paste. Combine paste and remaining ingredients in a large bowl and stir together until combined. Transfer into pie crust and cover with top crust. Flute edges of pie crust and prick top crust. Place pie on a large cookie sheet.

Bake at 450°F for 10 to 15 minutes, then reduce heat to 350°F. Bake an additional 45 to 55 minutes until golden brown and juice bubbles from top crust. Cool before serving.

Yields 8 to 10 servings.

If desired, decoratively sprinkle a mixture of 2 teaspoons sugar and 1/8 teaspoon freshly ground cinnamon lightly over top crust before baking.

Pies and Tarts

Naked Granny Apple Pie

Granny Smith goes topless and breaks many a taboo in this decadent crossbreed of cheesecake and deep-dish single-crust apple pie.

1 **Basic Pie Crust**
1 (8-ounce) package cream cheese, softened
1/2 cup sour cream
2 large eggs, beaten
1/2 cup lightly packed light brown sugar
1 tablespoon pure vanilla extract
1 teaspoon freshly squeezed lemon juice
1/2 teaspoon brandy
Pinch of freshly ground cinnamon
3 large or 4 small Granny Smith apples, peeled and sliced 1/4 inch thick,
   divided
2 tablespoons crushed almonds

Preheat oven to 450°F. Line a deep-dish pie pan with **Basic Pie Crust**.

With electric mixer on slow speed, beat cream cheese until smooth. Add remaining ingredients, except apples and almonds. Beat until smooth.

Set aside 12 apple slices. Stir remaining apples into filling and pour into lined pie dish. Press reserved apple slices onto top of filling and sprinkle with crushed almonds. Place pie on a large cookie sheet.

Bake at 450°F for 10 minutes, then reduce heat to 350°F. Bake an additional 45 to 50 minutes or until filling is firm and apples are very tender. Cool before serving.

Yields 8 to 10 servings.

Pies and Tarts

Crumble-Top Apple Pie

Topping:

1/2 cup walnuts

1-1/2 cups quick-cooking rolled oats

1/2 cup lightly packed light brown sugar

2 tablespoons all-purpose or whole wheat flour

Generous pinch of freshly ground cinnamon

3 tablespoons freshly squeezed lemon juice

1 tablespoon pure vanilla extract

1/2 cup vegetable oil

Filling:

1 **Basic Pie Crust**

2 tablespoons cornstarch

Freshly squeezed juice of 1/2 lemon

2 teaspoons pure vanilla extract

2 teaspoons brandy

4 large Granny Smith apples (about 4-1/2 cups), peeled and cut into 1/4-inch slices

1-1/4 cups sugar

4 tablespoons vegan margarine, chopped into small pieces

1 tablespoon all-purpose flour

1/4 teaspoon freshly ground cinnamon

To prepare topping: Grind walnuts finely in food processor. Add oats and grind slightly. In a medium mixing bowl, combine oats, nuts, and remaining dry ingredients. Add lemon juice, vanilla extract, and oil and stir until combined; set aside.

To prepare filling: Preheat oven to 450°F. Line a deep-dish pie pan with **Basic Pie Crust**.

In a small mixing bowl, thoroughly blend cornstarch, lemon juice, vanilla extract, and brandy into a paste. Combine paste and remaining ingredients in a large bowl and stir together until combined. Transfer into lined pie dish and spread topping over filling. Gently press down on topping until lightly packed. Place pie on a large cookie sheet.

Bake at 450°F for 10 minutes, then reduce to 350°F. Bake an additional 45 to 55 minutes or until golden brown and juice bubbles beneath topping. Cool before serving.

Yields 8 to 10 servings.

Pies and Tarts

Pecan Pie

I Basic Pie Crust
1/3 cup melted butter
I cup sugar
I cup light corn syrup
3 large eggs, beaten
1/8 teaspoon salt
I teaspoon pure vanilla extract
I teaspoon brandy
1-1/2 cups pecan halves or pieces

Preheat oven to 375°F. Line a deep-dish pie pan with **Basic Pie Crust**.

In a large mixing bowl, beat together butter, sugar, and corn syrup. Beat in eggs and stir in remaining ingredients. Pour into pie crust. Place pie on a large cookie sheet.

Bake 50 to 55 minutes until crust is lightly browned, filling is dark brown, and a toothpick inserted into center comes out clean. Cool completely before serving.

Yields 8 to 10 servings.

To enjoy Butterscotch Pecan Pie—as seen on *The Andy Griffith Show*—omit vanilla extract and add 2/3 cup butterscotch morsels. For Chocolate Pecan Pie, add 3/4 cup semisweet chocolate chips to the basic recipe. To really go wild, enhance the chocolate version with a tasty addition of I scant teaspoon instant coffee powder.

Almond Coffee Crunch Pie

1 **Basic Pie Crust**
1 generous tablespoon instant coffee powder
2 teaspoons pure vanilla extract
2 teaspoons brandy
1/3 cup melted butter
1 cup sugar
1 cup light corn syrup
3 large eggs, beaten
1-1/2 cups slivered almonds

Preheat oven to 375°F. Line a deep-dish pie pan with **Basic Pie Crust**.

In a small mixing bowl, thoroughly blend coffee powder, vanilla extract, and brandy into a paste. In a medium mixing bowl, beat together butter, sugar, and corn syrup. Beat in eggs. Combine all filling ingredients until fully combined and pour into pie crust. Place pie on a large cookie sheet.

Bake 50 to 55 minutes until crust is lightly browned, filling is dark brown, and a toothpick inserted into center comes out clean. Cool completely before serving.

Yields 8 to 10 servings.

"The Grit has rocked for a long time. Their support for art is second only to the food. I had a show there once, and traded a drawing for $35 credit. That drawing—of a cup of coffee—is still hanging at The Grit today."
—MICHAEL LACHOWSKI, PYLON

Pies and Tarts

Pies and Tarts

Lime-in-da-Coconut Pie

This deep-dish single-crust pie is a wonderful candidate for the clever practice of using finely ground graham cracker crumbs in place of flour when rolling out the crust.

I **Basic Pie Crust**
1-3/4 cups sour cream
1-3/4 cups sugar
1-1/2 cups sweetened flaked coconut
4 egg yolks, beaten
I tablespoon plain yellow cornmeal
I tablespoon pure vanilla extract
Pinch of salt
1/3 cup freshly squeezed lime juice

Preheat oven to 400°F. Line a deep-dish pie pan with **Basic Pie Crust**.

Thoroughly blend remaining ingredients and pour into pie crust. Place pie on a large baking sheet.

Bake approximately 1 hour or until the center of the pie is slightly brown on top and gently bubbling. Cool completely. Serve with sweetened whipped cream.

Yields 8 to 10 servings.

Sweet Potato Pie

I **Basic Pie Crust**
4 large sweet potatoes (enough to yield 3 cups when roasted and mashed)
I (14-ounce) can sweetened condensed milk
2 large eggs, beaten
Freshly squeezed juice of 1/2 lemon
I packed tablespoon light brown sugar
I teaspoon pure vanilla extract
I teaspoon brandy
Pinch of freshly ground cinnamon

Choose sweet potatoes with bright orange flesh and roast on a cookie sheet, in skins, in preheated 425°F oven until extremely soft and releasing caramelized juice, about 1 hour. Cool, peel, and measure, removing stringy and caramelized bits.

Preheat oven to 425°F. Line a deep-dish pie pan with **Basic Pie Crust**.

Blend all filling ingredients together with hand mixer. Beat until smooth. Remove stringy fibers caught on mixer blades. Transfer filling into lined pie dish. Place pie on a large cookie sheet.

Bake at 425°F for 15 minutes. Reduce heat to 350°F. Bake 45 to 55 minutes, until crust and top of pie filling are gently browned and a clean knife or toothpick inserted into the center comes out clean. Cool completely before serving.

Yields 8 to 10 servings.

Perhaps no other dish in the world is better paired with Sweetened Whipped Cream than this pie.

Sweetened Whipped Cream

I cup heavy whipping cream
3 tablespoons sugar
I teaspoon pure vanilla extract

In a very clean bowl, whip cream with electric mixer on high speed. As the cream gains volume, slowly add sugar. Continue whipping until stiff peaks form, but not until dry. Add vanilla extract and beat to combine.

Pies and Tarts

Cheesecake-Style Pumpkin Pie

1 **Basic Pie Crust**
1 (8-ounce) package cream cheese, softened
1/2 cup sugar
1/2 cup lightly packed light brown sugar
2 cups pumpkin puree
2 large eggs plus 1 yolk, beaten
3 tablespoons freshly squeezed lemon juice
2 teaspoons brandy
1 teaspoon pure vanilla extract
1/4 teaspoon freshly ground cinnamon
Pinch of salt
Pinch of freshly ground nutmeg
Very small pinch of freshly ground clove

Preheat oven to 425°F. Line a deep-dish pie pan with **Basic Pie Crust**.

With electric mixer on slow speed, beat cream cheese until smooth. Add sugars and beat until smooth. Combine all filling ingredients and blend until fully combined. Pour filling into crust. Place pie on a large cookie sheet.

Bake at 425°F for 15 minutes, then reduce heat to 350°F. Bake 40 to 45 minutes until crust and top of filling are lightly browned and a toothpick inserted in center comes out clean. Cool completely before serving.

Yields 8 to 10 servings.

Chocolate Eclair Pie

A deep-dish single-crust pie with a pastry cream filling and a rich topping.

Filling:
2/3 cup sugar
1/4 cup cornstarch
1/4 teaspoon salt
2-1/2 cups whole milk
5 large egg yolks
3 tablespoons butter, chopped into
   small pieces
2 teaspoons pure vanilla extract
1 teaspoon brandy
1 **Basic Pie Crust**, prebaked and
   cooled completely

Topping:
1 generous cup semisweet chocolate
   chips
3/4 cup sour cream

To prepare filling: Combine sugar, cornstarch, and salt in saucepan and whisk together thoroughly. Whisk milk in gradually. Add egg yolks and whisk until completely combined and mixture is even in color.

Place saucepan over medium heat, whisking continuously and scraping sides and bottom of pan, until mixture begins to simmer. Remove from heat. Whisk until very smooth. Return to medium heat, whisking continuously until mixture simmers again. Whisk well for 1 minute at simmer. Remove from heat and whisk in butter, vanilla extract, and brandy.

Before the filling has cooled completely, pour it into cooled pie shell. Cool to room temperature and refrigerate.

To prepare topping: Combine chocolate chips with sour cream in saucepan over gentle heat. Stir until chips soften and blend until smooth. Gently spread topping over prepared pie filling and refrigerate 2 hours or until firm.

Yields 8 to 10 servings.

For a delicious Butterscotch Eclair Pie, substitute butterscotch morsels for the chocolate chips in the topping.

Pies and Tarts

Sour Cream Chocolate Tart

Crust:
1 cup all-purpose flour
1/2 cup sugar
1/4 teaspoon salt
1/2 cup (1 stick) butter, chilled and
    chopped into small pieces
1 large egg
1 teaspoon whole milk
1 teaspoon pure vanilla extract

Filling:
3/4 cup semisweet chocolate chips
1-1/2 cups sour cream
1 egg, beaten
1/2 cup sugar
1 teaspoon pure vanilla extract

To prepare crust: In a medium mixing bowl, whisk together flour, sugar, and salt. Cut butter into flour mixture with pastry blender until particles are very small, approximately 1/4 the size of a chocolate chip. Beat together egg, milk, and vanilla and add to flour mixture. Toss together until liquid is fully integrated and mixture can be formed into a ball. Press dough evenly into an 8- or 9-inch removable-bottom tart pan with fluted rim. Press dough approximately 1-1/4 inches up sides of pan and place in refrigerator while preparing filling.

To prepare filling: Preheat oven to 375°F.

Combine chocolate chips and 1 heaping tablespoon of sour cream in saucepan. Warm gently over low heat until chocolate is soft and can be blended.

With electric mixer on medium speed, beat together all ingredients until very smooth. Spread into chilled crust. Place pie on a large cookie sheet.

Bake 35 to 40 minutes or until crust is well browned and center of tart jiggles when gently shaken. Cool completely before serving.

Yields 8 to 10 servings.

French Coffee Cream Delight

Pies and Tarts

A sibling to our **Sour Cream Chocolate Tart**.

Crust:
- 1 cup all-purpose flour
- 1/2 cup sugar
- 1/4 teaspoon salt
- 1/2 cup (1 stick) butter, chilled and chopped into small pieces
- 1 large egg
- 1 teaspoon whole milk
- 1 teaspoon pure vanilla extract

Filling:
- 2 teaspoons instant coffee powder
- 2 teaspoons pure vanilla extract
- 1 large egg, beaten
- 1-1/2 cups sour cream
- 2/3 cup sugar
- 1/2 cup chocolate chips

To prepare crust: Whisk together flour, sugar, and salt. Cut butter into flour mixture with pastry blender until particles are very small, approximately 1/4 the size of a chocolate chip. Beat together egg, milk, and vanilla extract and add to flour mixture. Toss together until liquid is fully integrated and mixture can be formed into a ball. Press dough evenly into an 8- or 9-inch removable-bottom tart pan. Form dough approximately 1-1/4 inches up sides of pan and place in refrigerator while preparing filling.

To prepare filling: Preheat oven to 375°F.

Blend instant coffee powder with vanilla extract. With electric mixer on medium speed, blend all ingredients except chocolate chips until very smooth. Spread into chilled crust. Distribute chocolate chips evenly over surface of filling. Lightly press chocolate chips into filling until just immersed. Place pie on a large cookie sheet.

Bake 35 to 40 minutes or until crust is well browned and center of tart jiggles when gently shaken. Cool completely before serving.

Yields 8 to 10 servings.

Pies and Tarts

White Chocolate Decadence Pie

Crust:
2 cups very finely ground vanilla wafer crumbs
6 tablespoons (3/4 stick) butter, melted

Filling:
1 cup heavy whipping cream, divided
12 ounces cream cheese, softened
1/2 cup sugar
1 tablespoon pure vanilla
1/2 cup (generous) or 2/3 cup white chocolate morsels
Caramel sauce, white chocolate morsels, cookie crumbs to garnish.

To prepare crust: Preheat oven to 350°F.

Place vanilla wafer crumbs (which are easily prepared in a food processor) in a large bowl and stir in melted butter. Use a spoon to blend ingredients until uniform, then use your hands to combine crumbs and butter as thoroughly as possible.

In a deep dish pie pan or glass dish, form a thick crust with the crumb mixture. Begin by packing crumbs densely to form a firm crust on the bottom of the dish. Reserve enough crumbs to form equally thick and firm sides. A flat-bottomed drinking glass can be used to pack crumbs, but hands work fine; they may be a bit sore if you do a good job (press hard)! There is an art to this but you can achieve a good, crunchy result if you apply yourself.

Place crust-lined dish into oven and bake 10 minutes. Remove and allow to cool. Refrigerate until chilled.

To prepare filling: Reserve 1/4 cup of heavy whipping cream and set aside. Using a very clean, chilled bowl and chilled beaters, whip remaining 3/4 cup heavy whipping cream with an electric mixer on high speed until stiff peaks form, but not until dry. Set aside in refrigerator.

In a mixing bowl, thoroughly cream together softened cream cheese and sugar. Beat in vanilla extract.

Combine measured white chocolate morsels and reserved 1/4 cup heavy whipping cream in a saucepan over gentle heat or in a bowl in a microwave, and heat just until soft enough to blend. Mix thoroughly into cream cheese mixture. Stir in whipped cream and blend until uniform, scraping sides of bowl to mix thoroughly. Spoon filling into chilled crust, drizzle with caramel sauce, and sprinkle with crumbled white chocolate morsels and cookie crumbs. Refrigerate until well chilled before serving.

Yields 8 to 10 servings.

Pies and Tarts

Pies and Tarts

Creamy Coconut Rum and Cashew Butter Silk Pie

Best when refrigerated several hours prior to serving. Then whammo! A one-of-a-kind, weirdly wonderful treat.

Crust:
2 cups very finely ground vanilla wafer crumbs
6 tablespoons (3/4 stick) butter, melted

Filling:
1 cup heavy whipping cream, divided
12 ounces cream cheese, softened
1 cup packed light brown sugar
1 tablespoon coconut rum
1 teaspoon pure vanilla extract
1/3 cup cashew buter (available at most natural food stores)

To prepare crust: Preheat oven to 350°F.

Place vanilla wafer crumbs (which are easily prepared in a food processor) in a large bowl and stir in melted butter. Use a spoon to blend ingredients until uniform, then use your hands to combine crumbs and butter as thoroughly as possible.

In a deep-dish pie pan or glass dish, form a thick crust with the crumb mixture. Begin by packing crumbs densely to form a firm crust on the bottom of the dish. Conserve enough crumbs to form equally thick and firm sides. A flat-bottomed drinking glass can be used to pack crumbs, but hands work fine; they may be a bit sore if you do a good job (press hard)! There is an art to this but you can achieve a good, crunchy result if you apply yourself.

Place crust-lined dish into oven and bake 10 minutes. Remove and allow to cool. Refrigerate until chilled.

Using a very clean, chilled bowl and chilled beaters, whip heavy cream with an electric beater on high speed until stiff peaks form, but not until dry. Set aside in refrigerator.

In a mixing bowl, thoroughly cream together cream cheese and light brown sugar. Add coconut rum, vanilla extract, and cashew butter. Beat together, then add whipped cream and mix until thoroughly combined, scraping the sides of the bowl with a rubber spatula. When fully blended, spoon filling into chilled crust, use a fork to make decorative marks on top, and/or sprinkle with cookie crumbs. Refrigerate at least 2 hours before serving.

Yields 8 to 10 servings.

Pies and Tarts

A Bunch of Layer Cakes and One Fine Cheesecake

- **Grit Cream Cheese Icing**
- **Grit Vegan Buttercream Frosting**
- **Amaretto Cream Cake**
- **Grit Carrot Cake**
- **Vegan Carrot Cake**
- **Orange Creamsicle Cake**
- **Vanilla Malted Cake**
- **Lil' Jim's Puddin' Cake**
- **Milk Chocolate Toasted Coconut Cake**
- **Mint Chocolate Chip Grasshopper Cake**
- **Peanut Butter Chocolate Cake**
- **Cocoacoconut Cake**
- **Deep Dark Chocolate Cake**
- **Dark Chocolate Cake with Cream Cheese Icing**
- **Chocolate Vegan Death Cake**
- **Caramel Layer Cake**
- **Butterscotch Pumpkin Cheesecake**

Grit Cream Cheese Icing

A basic appeal of many cakes at The Grit is the richness of our cream cheese icing. It's made with top-notch cream cheese and applied generously. Here is the simple icing that crowns such favorites as **Grit Carrot Cake** and **Dark Chocolate Cake with Grit Cream Cheese Icing** (you know, the one with cookies poking out of the top). It is also a luxurious starting point for several flavorful variations to follow.

2 (8-ounce) packages cream cheese, slightly softened and cut into small pieces
1/2 cup (1 stick) butter, at room temperature
4 cups powdered confectioners' sugar, sifted
2 teaspoons pure vanilla extract

Using an electric mixer, beat cream cheese in a large bowl until smooth. Add butter and beat until smooth, creamy, and fully combined. Add powdered confectioners' sugar and vanilla extract and beat slowly until sugar is incorporated. Continue to beat until consistency is extremely smooth and fluffy.

Yields icing for 3 (9-inch) cake layers.

"I eat at The Grit so often I can almost quote the menu. I think I'm obsessed."

—JENNIFER NETTLES,
JENNIFER NETTLES BAND

Grit Vegan Buttercream Frosting

With delightful bonus variations to boot.

> 1 cup vegan margarine, softened
> 2 (1-pound) boxes powdered confectioners' sugar (approximately 6 cups)
> 1 teaspoon pure vanilla extract
> 2 to 3 tablespoons soymilk or water

Using an electric mixer, beat margarine in a large bowl until thoroughly creamed. Add sugar 1 cup at a time, beating well after each addition, and scrape bottom and sides of bowl with a rubber spatula to ensure thorough mixing. Blend in vanilla, followed by enough soy milk or water to create a desirable, lightly spreadable, but firm consistency. Voilà!

Variations on this frosting include:

Peanut Butter Frosting
Blend 2 tablespoons of peanut butter into margarine before adding sugar.

Chocolate Vegan Buttercream Frosting
Blend 1/2 cup cocoa powder into frosting.

Mocha Vegan Buttercream Frosting
Dissolve 2 tablespoons instant coffee into 1 tablespoon pure vanilla extract, and blend into frosting with 2 tablespoons cocoa powder.

Yields icing for 3 (9-inch) cake layers.

A Bunch of Layer Cakes and One Fine Cheesecake

A Bunch of Layer Cakes and One Fine Cheesecake

Amaretto Cream Cake

If it's been years since you've engaged in any activities involving maraschino cherries, your time has arrived. Try this delight with a syrup of sweet almond liqueur inside and garnished with neon red cherries on top.

Cake:
3 cups sifted cake flour
1 tablespoon double-acting baking powder
1/2 teaspoon salt
1 cup whole milk, at room temperature
1/4 cup vegetable oil
1 teaspoon pure vanilla extract
1 cup (2 sticks) butter, at room temperature
2 cups sugar
4 eggs, at room temperature

Syrup:
1/2 cup water
1/3 cup amaretto liqueur
2 tablespoons sugar
1 tablespoon vanilla extract

Icing:
2-1/2 cups heavy whipping cream
1/2 cup sugar
2 teaspoons amaretto liqueur
1/4 teaspoon vanilla extract
12 maraschino cherries, drained and dried on a paper towel

To prepare cake: Preheat oven to 350°F. Grease 3 (9-inch) round cake pans, dust with flour, and line bottom with parchment or wax paper.

Sift flour, baking powder, and salt. Blend milk, oil, and vanilla extract. In a large mixing bowl with electric mixer on medium speed, cream together butter and sugar until light and fluffy. Add eggs 1 at a time, beating well after each addition.

Add flour mixture to butter mixture alternately with milk mixture, beating just until smooth after each addition.

Divide batter evenly into prepared pans.

Bake 25 minutes or just until a knife or toothpick inserted in the center of layers comes out clean. Remove from oven, cool on a wire rack for 10 minutes, then remove from pans. Allow layers to cool completely before drizzling with syrup and covering with icing.

To prepare syrup: Combine ingredients in saucepan and bring to a boil for 1 full minute.

Remove from heat. Turn cooled cake layers upside down and slightly scuff bottom surface. Lightly and evenly drizzle 1/3 of syrup onto layers and allow to soak in. Apply only enough syrup to lightly moisten but not drench layers. Handle soaked layers very gently while icing and stacking.

To prepare icing: In a very clean bowl, begin whipping cream with electric mixer on high speed. As cream gains volume, slowly add sugar. When soft peaks form, slowly add amaretto and vanilla, and continue whipping until stiff but not dry.

Frost between layers, and top and sides of cake. Decorate with a ring of cherries.

Yields 10 to 12 servings.

"The Grit is the last place I eat before I go tour and the first place I eat when I get back."
—ORENDA FINK,
LITTLE RED ROCKET

A Bunch of Layer Cakes and One Fine Cheesecake

A Bunch of Layer Cakes and One Fine Cheesecake

Grit Carrot Cake

Smothered in rich cream cheese icing and towering ludicrously high behind the glass of our dessert case, **Grit Carrot Cake** is beloved for its nutty, chewy filling, especially the distinctive dried sweet cranberries.

Cake:
3 cups sifted all-purpose flour

2 teaspoons freshly ground cinnamon

1-1/2 teaspoons double-acting baking powder

1-1/2 teaspoons baking soda

1-1/2 teaspoons salt

Generous pinch of freshly ground nutmeg

Pinch of freshly ground clove

6 beaten eggs, at room temperature

3 cups sugar

2 cups vegetable oil

4 cups shredded carrots

1-1/4 cups finely chopped walnuts

1 generous cup dried sweetened cranberries

Icing:
1 batch **Grit Cream Cheese Icing**

To prepare cake: Preheat oven to 350°F. Grease 3 (9-inch) round cake pans, dust with flour, and line bottom with parchment or wax paper.

Sift together flour, baking powder, salt, nutmeg, and clove in a large bowl. Thoroughly mix eggs, sugar, and vegetable oil and stir together with flour mixture until fully combined. Add carrots, walnuts, and cranberries and stir until fully combined. Divide batter evenly into prepared pans.

Bake 30 to 35 minutes or just until a knife or toothpick inserted in the center of layers comes out clean. Remove from oven, cool 15 to 20 minutes on a wire rack, and remove from pans. Allow layers to cool completely before icing.

Icing the cake: Frost between layers, and top and sides of cake. Sprinkle lightly with crushed walnuts on top.

Yields 10 to 12 servings.

This dark-colored cake has a large crumb which sometimes comes loose and can show through the white icing. It may be useful to apply a crumb coating— a very thin initial coating of icing to trap crumbs. After applying, place cake in the freezer for a few minutes to solidify crumb coat and proceed with a clean, crumb-free spatula to decorate cake with remaining icing.

Vegan Carrot Cake

Milk and eggs might make you wary, so just don't put 'em in. Who said that being vegan means you're not allowed to sin?

Cake:

3-1/3 cups all-purpose flour	2 cups sweetened shredded coconut
1 tablespoon baking soda	1-1/2 cups vegetable oil
1 tablespoon cinnamon	1 (20-ounce) can crushed pineapple in juice
1-1/2 teaspoons salt	
1-1/2 teaspoons pumpkin pie spice or allspice	2/3 cup water
	2 teaspoons pure vanilla
1 cup plus 2 tablespoons light brown sugar	1 cup raisins or dried sweetened cranberries (optional)
1 cup plus 2 tablespoons white sugar	1 cup chopped walnuts (optional)
3 cups shredded carrots	

Icing:
1 batch **Grit Vegan Buttercream Frosting**

To prepare cake: Preheat oven to 350°F. Grease 3 (9-inch) round cake pans, dust with flour, and line bottoms with parchment or wax paper.

Sift flour, baking soda, spices, and salt together into a large mixing bowl. Add sugars and thoroughly combine with dry mixture. Add all remaining ingredients and stir together thoroughly until mixture is uniform. Use a rubber spatula to scrape sides of bowl. If the batter appears too thick, a small amount of additional water maybe be mixed in. When thoroughly blended to desired consistency, divide batter evenly into prepared pans.

Bake for 30 to 35 minutes or just until a clean knife or toothpick inserted in center of layers comes out clean. Remove from oven and cool 10 minutes on a wire rack. Remove from pans and allow layers to cool completely before icing.

Icing the cake: Frost between layers, and top and sides of cake with **Grit Vegan Buttercream Frosting**. And please see page 152 for special instructions at the bottom of the page for applying a "Crumb Coating" to large-crumbed, dark cake layers.

Yields 10 to 12 servings.

A Bunch of Layer Cakes and One Fine Cheesecake

A Bunch of Layer
Cakes and One
Fine Cheesecake

Orange Creamsicle Cake

A batch of **Grit Cream Cheese Icing** undergoes a clever twist to frost and fill this cake with a flavor familiar from childhood.

Cake:
- 1 cup (2 sticks) butter, at room temperature
- 2 cups sugar
- 4 eggs, at room temperature
- 3 cups sifted cake flour
- 1 tablespoon double-acting baking powder
- 1/2 teaspoon salt
- 1 cup whole milk, at room temperature
- 1/4 cup vegetable oil
- 1 teaspoon pure vanilla extract

Filling:
- 1 cup **Grit Cream Cheese Icing**
- 3 tablespoons orange juice concentrate
- 2 tablespoons brandy

Icing:
- 3 cups **Grit Cream Cheese Icing**
- 1 tablespoon plus 2 teaspoons orange juice concentrate
- 12 Pirouline cookies or vanilla wafers

To prepare cake: Preheat oven to 350°F. Grease 3 (9-inch) round cake pans, dust with flour, and line bottom with parchment or wax paper.

In a large mixing bowl with electric mixer on medium speed, cream together butter and sugar until light and fluffy. Add eggs 1 at a time, beating well after each addition. Sift flour with baking powder and salt. Blend milk with oil and vanilla extract.

Add flour mixture to butter mixture alternately with milk mixture, beating after each addition just until smooth. Divide batter evenly into prepared pans.

Bake 25 minutes or just until a clean knife or toothpick inserted in the center of layers comes out clean. Remove from oven, cool 10 minutes on a wire rack. Remove from pans and allow layers to cool completely before icing.

To prepare filling: Combine ingredients and stir to a loose custard-like consistency. Frost between inside layers and, if you possess the manual dexterity to do so, slice layers through the center, frost inside, and put back together. Stack layers one atop the other with filling alternating.

Icing the cake: Blend ingredients together and frost top and sides of filled, stacked layers. Garnish with a ring of Pirouline cookies or vanilla wafers inserted in top of cake.

Yields 10 to 12 servings.

Vanilla Malted Cake

It's like a shake, but it's a cake.

Cake:
- 1 cup (2 sticks) butter, at room temperature
- 2 cups sugar
- 4 eggs, at room temperature
- 3 cups sifted cake flour
- 1 tablespoon double-acting baking powder
- 1/2 teaspoon salt
- 1 cup whole milk, at room temperature
- 1/4 cup vegetable oil
- 1 teaspoon pure vanilla extract

Syrup:
- 1/2 cup malted milk powder
- 1/2 cup water
- 3 tablespoons brandy
- 2 tablespoons pure vanilla extract
- 1 teaspoon sugar

Icing:
- 4 tablespoons malted milk powder
- Pure vanilla extract
- 1 batch **Grit Cream Cheese Icing**

To prepare cake: Preheat oven to 350°F. Grease 3 (9-inch) round cake pans, dust with flour, and line bottom with parchment or wax paper.

In a large mixing bowl with electric mixer on medium speed, cream together butter and sugar until light and fluffy. Add eggs 1 at a time, beating well after each addition. Sift together flour, baking powder, and salt. Blend together milk, oil, and vanilla extract.

Add flour mixture to butter mixture alternately with milk mixture, beating after each addition just until smooth. Divide batter evenly into prepared pans.

Bake 25 minutes or just until a knife or toothpick inserted in the center of layers comes out clean. Remove from oven, cool 10 minutes on a wire rack. Remove from pans and allow layers to cool completely before icing.

To prepare syrup: Combine ingredients in saucepan and bring to a boil for 1 minute. Remove from heat. Turn cooled cake layers upside down and slightly scuff bottom surface. Lightly and evenly drizzle 1/3 of syrup onto layers and allow to soak in. Apply only enough syrup to lightly moisten but not drench layers. Handle soaked layers very gently while icing and stacking.

To prepare icing: Blend malted milk powder with enough vanilla extract to form thick paste. Mix with icing until fully combined. Frost between layers, and top and sides of cake.

Yields 10 to 12 servings.

A Bunch of Layer Cakes and One Fine Cheesecake

A Bunch of Layer
Cakes and One
Fine Cheesecake

Lil' Jim's Puddin' Cake

Cake:
4-1/2 cups all-purpose flour
3 cups sugar
I cup cocoa powder
I tablespoon baking soda
2 teaspoons salt
1-1/2 cups vegetable oil
2 tablespoons pure vanilla extract
3 cups strong brewed coffee
1/4 cup cider vinegar

Icing:
2 cups heavy whipping cream
6 tablespoons sugar
2 teaspoons pure vanilla extract

Pastry Cream Filling:
1/3 cup sugar
2 tablespoons cornstarch
1/8 teaspoon salt
1-1/4 cups whole milk
3 small egg yolks
1-1/2 tablespoons butter, chopped
   into small pieces
I teaspoon pure vanilla extract
I teaspoon brandy

To prepare cake: Preheat oven to 350°F. Grease 3 (9-inch) round cake pans, dust with flour, and line bottom with parchment or wax paper.

Sift together dry ingredients in a large bowl. Add oil and vanilla extract. With electric mixer on low speed, blend until fully combined. With mixer on medium speed, gradually blend in coffee. When mixture is smooth, add vinegar and blend on low speed just until combined. Divide batter evenly into prepared pans.

Bake 20 to 25 minutes or just until a knife or toothpick inserted in the center of layers comes out clean. Remove from oven, cool 15 to 20 minutes on a wire rack. Remove from pans and allow layers to cool completely before icing.

To prepare pastry cream filling: Combine sugar, cornstarch, and salt in saucepan and whisk together thoroughly. Whisk milk in gradually. Add egg yolks and whisk until completely combined and mixture is even in color.

Place saucepan over medium heat, whisking continuously and scraping sides and bottom of pan, until mixture begins to simmer. Remove from heat. Whisk until very smooth.

Return to medium heat, whisking continuously until mixture simmers again. Whisk well for a full minute at simmer. Remove from heat and whisk in butter, vanilla extract, and brandy. Cool to room temperature, then refrigerate.

Generously frost tops of two cake layers with pastry cream. (Since chocolate cake layers can be very smooth and glossy, it is best to scuff or remove a thin layer from top of inside layers to prevent sliding during handling and cutting.) Stack frosted cake layers one atop the other and top with unfrosted cake layer.

To prepare icing: In a very clean bowl, whip cream with electric mixer on high speed. As the cream gains volume, slowly add sugar. Continue whipping until stiff peaks form, but not until dry. Add vanilla extract and beat to combine. Frost top and sides of cake.

Yields 10 to 12 servings.

Milk Chocolate Toasted Coconut Cake

Cake:

3 cups sifted cake flour

1 tablespoon double-acting baking powder

1/2 teaspoon salt

1/4 cup vegetable oil

1 cup chocolate syrup, at room temperature

1 teaspoon pure vanilla extract

1 cup (2 sticks) butter, at room temperature

1-1/2 cups sugar

4 large eggs, at room temperature

Icing:

3 cups gently packed sweetened coconut flakes

1 batch **Grit Cream Cheese Icing**

A Bunch of Layer Cakes and One Fine Cheesecake

A Bunch of Layer Cakes and One Fine Cheesecake

To prepare cake: Preheat oven to 350°F. Grease 3 (9-inch) round cake pans, dust with flour, and line bottom with parchment or wax paper.

Sift flour, baking powder, and salt; set aside. Blend oil, chocolate syrup, and vanilla extract; set aside. In a large mixing bowl using an electric mixer on medium speed, cream together butter and sugar until light and fluffy. Add eggs 1 at a time, beating well after each addition.

Add flour mixture to butter mixture alternately with chocolate mixture, beating after each addition just until smooth. Divide batter evenly into prepared pans.

Bake 25 minutes or just until a knife or toothpick inserted in the center of layers comes out clean. Remove from oven, cool 10 minutes on a wire rack. Remove from pans and allow layers to cool completely before icing.

To prepare icing: Preheat oven to 350°F.

Spread coconut into thin layer on ungreased sheet pan. Toast until golden brown, turning periodically. Remove from oven and scatter on a plate to cool.

Frost between layers, and top and sides of cake. Gently apply a light coating of toasted coconut to top and sides of frosted cake.

Yields 10 to 12 servings.

"How cool is it that our drummer's girlfriend works at The Grit?!"

—ADAM DURITZ, COUNTING CROWS

Mint Chocolate Chip Grasshopper Cake

Cake:
4-1/2 cups all-purpose flour
3 cups sugar
1 cup cocoa powder
1 tablespoon baking soda
2 teaspoons salt
1-1/2 cups vegetable oil
2 tablespoons vanilla extract
3 cups strong brewed coffee
1/4 cup cider vinegar

Icing:
1-1/2 cups chocolate chips
1 batch **Grit Cream Cheese Icing**
1 tablespoon mint extract
Green food coloring
Chocolate chips or chocolate
   shavings, to decorate

To prepare cake: Preheat oven to 350°F. Grease 3 (9-inch) round cake pans, dust with flour, and line bottom with parchment or wax paper.

Sift together dry ingredients in a large bowl. Add oil and vanilla extract. With electric mixer on low speed, blend until fully combined. With mixer on medium speed, gradually blend in coffee. When mixture is smooth, add vinegar and blend on low speed just until combined. Divide batter evenly into prepared pans.

Bake 20 to 25 minutes or just until a knife or toothpick inserted in the center of layers comes out clean. Remove from oven, cool 15 to 20 minutes on a wire rack. Remove from pans and allow layers to fully cool before icing.

To prepare icing: Place chocolate chips in food processor and pulse just until broken into very small pieces. Combine with cream cheese icing, mint extract, and enough food coloring to give icing a very bright, vibrant green color. Mix until fully blended. Frost between layers, and top and sides of cake. Decorate as desired with chocolate chips or chocolate shavings.

Yields 10 to 12 servings.

Chocolate Shavings

To make chocolate shavings, draw a vegetable peeler or cheese slicer across the thin edge of a block of best-quality white or milk chocolate. Hold the chocolate with a paper towel folded into quarters to protect it from the heat of your hand and allow the shavings to fall onto a piece of parchment or wax paper. (Generally, room-temperature or very slightly warmed chocolate will yield long curls and chilled chocolate will give small shavings.) Refrigerate until ready to use.

A Bunch of Layer Cakes and One Fine Cheesecake

Peanut Butter Chocolate Cake

Cake:
4-1/2 cups all-purpose flour
3 cups sugar
1 cup cocoa powder
1 tablespoon baking soda
2 teaspoons salt
1-1/2 cups vegetable oil
2 tablespoons pure vanilla extract
3 cups strong brewed coffee
1/4 cup cider vinegar

Icing:
1 batch **Grit Cream Cheese Icing**
1 cup smooth peanut butter
1/4 cup semisweet chocolate chips, melted
1/8 cup cocoa powder, to decorate

To prepare cake: Preheat oven to 350°F. Grease 3 (9-inch) round cake pans, dust with flour, and line bottom with parchment or wax paper.

Sift together dry ingredients in a large bowl. Add oil and vanilla extract. With electric mixer on low speed, blend until fully combined. With mixer on medium speed, gradually blend in coffee. When mixture is smooth, add vinegar and blend on low speed just until combined. Divide batter evenly into prepared pans.

Bake 20 to 25 minutes or just until a knife or toothpick inserted in the center of layers comes out clean. Remove from oven, cool 15 to 20 minutes on a wire rack. Remove from pans and allow layers to cool completely before icing.

To prepare icing: Thoroughly combine icing, peanut butter, and melted chocolate chips. Frost between layers, and top and sides of cake and decorate with a light dusting of cocoa powder.

Yields 10 to 12 servings.

Cocoacoconut Cake

Cake:

2 cups sifted cake flour

1 cup cocoa powder

1 tablespoon double-acting baking powder

1/2 teaspoon salt

1 cup plus 1 tablespoon whole milk, at room temperature

1/4 cup vegetable oil

1 teaspoon pure vanilla extract

1 cup (2 sticks) butter, at room temperature

2 cups sugar

4 eggs, at room temperature

Icing:

1-3/4 cups semisweet chocolate chips

1 (14-ounce) can sweetened condensed milk

3/4 cup sour cream

4 cups gently packed sweetened coconut flakes

To prepare cake: Preheat oven to 350°F. Grease 3 (9-inch) round cake pans, dust with flour, and line bottom with parchment or wax paper.

Sift together flour, cocoa powder, baking powder, and salt. Blend milk, oil, and vanilla extract. In a large mixing bowl with electric mixer on medium speed, cream butter with sugar until light and fluffy. Add eggs 1 at a time, beating well after each addition.

Add flour mixture to butter mixture alternately with milk mixture, beating after each addition just until smooth. Divide batter evenly into prepared pans.

Bake 25 minutes or just until a knife or toothpick inserted in the center of layers comes out clean. Remove from oven, cool 10 minutes on a wire rack. Remove from pans and allow layers to cool completely before icing.

To prepare icing: Combine chocolate chips and condensed milk in saucepan over gentle heat and stir continuously until chocolate has melted completely. Remove from heat and stir in sour cream. Add coconut, stir until combined, and allow icing to cool slightly. Frost between layers, and top and sides of cake before icing has cooled completely.

Yields 10 to 12 servings.

A Bunch of Layer Cakes and One Fine Cheesecake

A Bunch of Layer
Cakes and One
Fine Cheesecake

Deep Dark Chocolate Cake

With just two ingredients (plus a little patience), this cake's simple ganache can be used for lots of other cakes and is multiplied easily for larger batches.

Cake:

2 cups sifted cake flour
1 cup cocoa powder
1 tablespoon double-acting baking powder
1/2 teaspoon salt
1 cup plus 1 tablespoon whole milk, at room temperature

1/4 cup vegetable oil
1 teaspoon pure vanilla extract
1 cup (2 sticks) butter, at room temperature
2 cups sugar
4 eggs, at room temperature

Chocolate Ganache:

2 cups heavy cream, preferably 40% milk fat
2 cups semisweet chocolate chips
Chocolate shavings, to decorate (optional)

To prepare cake: Preheat oven to 350°F. Grease 3 (9-inch) round cake pans, dust with flour, and line bottom with parchment or wax paper.

Sift together flour, cocoa powder, baking powder, and salt. Blend milk, oil, and vanilla extract. In a large mixing bowl with electric mixer on medium speed, cream together butter and sugar until light and fluffy. Add eggs 1 at a time, beating well after each addition.

Add flour mixture to butter mixture alternately with milk mixture, beating after each addition just until smooth. Divide batter evenly into prepared pans.

Bake 25 minutes or just until a knife or toothpick inserted in the center of layers comes out clean. Remove from oven, cool 10 minutes on a wire rack. Remove from pans and allow layers to cool completely before icing with chocolate ganache.

To prepare chocolate ganache: Heat cream in a saucepan, stirring often until hot. Add chocolate chips and stir until chips begin to melt. Transfer to food processor and puree into thick, glossy, dark liquid. Cool slightly and transfer to metal bowl. For immediate use, place in freezer and stir every 15 minutes until mixture thickens nearly to the consistency of peanut butter. For later use, transfer from food processor to sealable container and refrigerate for several hours or until mixture fully thickens.

Garnish with chocolate shavings, if desired.

Yields 10 to 12 servings.

Dark Chocolate Cake with Cream Cheese Icing

Cake:
4-1/2 cups all-purpose flour
3 cups sugar
1 cup cocoa powder
1 tablespoon baking soda
2 teaspoons salt
1-1/2 cups vegetable oil
2 tablespoons pure vanilla extract
3 cups strong brewed coffee
1/4 cup cider vinegar

Icing:
1 batch **Grit Cream Cheese Icing**
Chocolate kisses or cookies, for
  garnish

To prepare cake: Preheat oven to 350°F. Grease 3 (9-inch) round cake pans, dust with flour, and line bottom with parchment or wax paper.

Sift together dry ingredients in a large bowl. Add oil and vanilla extract. With electric mixer on low speed, blend until fully combined. With mixer on medium speed, gradually blend in coffee. When mixture is smooth, add vinegar and blend on low speed just until combined.

Divide batter evenly into prepared pans.

Bake for 20 to 25 minutes or just until a knife or toothpick inserted in the center of layers comes out clean. Remove from oven and cool 15 to 20 minutes on a wire rack. Remove from pans and allow layers to cool completely before icing.

To prepare icing: Frost layers with icing. Crumbs from this dark cake can sometimes come loose and show through the white icing. It may be useful to apply a crumb coating—a very thin initial coating of icing to trap crumbs. After applying, place cake in the freezer for a few minutes to solidify crumb coat and proceed with a clean, crumb-free spatula to decorate cake with remaining icing. Garnish with any dark chocolate candy or cookie inserted into or placed on top of cake in a circular design.

Yields 10 to 12 servings.

A Bunch of Layer Cakes and One Fine Cheesecake

A Bunch of Layer Cakes and One Fine Cheesecake

Chocolate Vegan Death Cake Ⓥ

Cake:
4-1/2 cups all-purpose flour
3 cups sugar
1 cup cocoa powder
1 tablespoon baking soda
2 teaspoons salt
1-1/2 cups vegetable oil
2 tablespoons pure vanilla extract
3 cups strong brewed coffee
1/4 cup cider vinegar

Icing:
1 (12-ounce) package firm silken tofu
3 cups vegan chocolate chips (many semisweet brands contain no dairy)

To prepare cake: Preheat oven to 350°F. Grease 3 (9-inch) round cake pans, dust with flour, and line bottom with parchment or wax paper.

Sift together dry ingredients in a large bowl. Add oil and vanilla extract. With electric mixer on low speed, blend until fully combined. With mixer on medium speed, gradually blend in coffee. When mixture is smooth, add vinegar and blend on low speed just until combined. Divide batter evenly into prepared pans.

Bake 20 to 25 minutes or just until a knife or toothpick inserted in the center of layers comes out clean. Remove from oven and cool 15 to 20 minutes on a wire rack. Remove from pans and allow layers to cool completely before icing.

To prepare icing: Drain excess fluid from silken tofu, crush and place in a medium saucepan with chocolate chips. Stir together over medium heat until chocolate is very soft. Transfer to food processor and puree until fully blended. Cool to spreadable consistency and frost between layers, and top and sides of cake.

Yields 10 to 12 servings.

Caramel Layer Cake

A confectionary conquistador of will power, calling out to its victims from behind the clear, cool glass of the Grit dessert case.

Cake:

1 cup shortening	1 teaspoon salt
1 cup white sugar	1 cup milk
1 cup dark brown sugar	3/4 cup vegetable oil
4 eggs, at room temperature	1 tablespoon vanilla extract
3 cups sifted all-purpose flour	3/4 cup water
1 tablespoon baking powder	

Icing:

1 batch **Grit Cream Cheese Icing**
2 tablespoons dark brown sugar
1 teaspoon pure vanilla extract

Alternate Icing:

2 cups heavy whipping cream
4 tablespoons white sugar
2 teaspoons vanilla extract
2 level, very lightly packed
   tablespoons dark brown sugar

To prepare cake: Preheat oven to 350°F. Grease 3 (9-inch) round cake pans, dust with flour, and line bottoms with parchment or wax paper.

In a large mixing bowl, with electric mixer on medium speed, cream together shortening, white sugar, and dark brown sugar until light and fluffy. Add eggs 1 at a time, beating well after each addition. Re-sift flour together with baking powder and salt. Blend milk with oil and vanilla extract.

Add flour mixture to shortening mixture alternately with milk mixture, beating after each addition just until smooth. Add water and beat just until smooth. Divide batter evenly into prepared pans.

Bake 25 minutes or just until a clean knife or toothpick inserted in the center of layers comes out clean. Remove from oven and cool 10 minutes on a wire rack. Remove from pans and allow layers to cool completely before icing.

A Bunch of Layer Cakes and One Fine Cheesecake

A Bunch of Layer Cakes and One Fine Cheesecake

To prepare icing: Blend **Grit Cream Cheese Icing** with additions until smooth. Frost between layers, and top and sides of cake.

To prepare alternate icing: Using a very clean, chilled bowl and chilled beaters, whip cream with an electric mixer on high speed. As the cream gains volume, slowly add white sugar. Continue whipping until stiff peaks form, but not until dry. Add vanilla extract and dark brown sugar and beat just until combined. Frost between layers, and top and sides of cake.

Yields 10 to 12 servings.

Butterscotch Pumpkin Cheesecake

Sounds great and tastes incredible.

Crust:
2-1/4 cups graham cracker crumbs
1/2 cup (1 stick) melted butter

Filling:
1/2 cup sour cream
1/2 cup butterscotch morsels
24 ounces cream cheese, softened
5 large eggs, at room temperature, beaten

1/2 cup canned pumpkin puree
1 cup sugar
1/4 cup all-purpose flour
1 teaspoon pure vanilla extract

Glaze:
1/2 cup packed light brown sugar
1/2 cup sour cream

To prepare crust: Stir crumbs and butter together and press evenly into bottom of 10 x 3-inch springform pan; set aside.

To prepare filling: Preheat oven to 350°F.

Combine sour cream and butterscotch morsels in saucepan over gentle heat. Stir until morsels soften and blend until smooth. In a large mixing bowl with electric mixer on medium speed, beat cream cheese until smooth. Combine remaining ingredients and beat until smooth. Pour into prepared crust. Place cheesecake on a large cookie sheet.

Bake 1 hour to 70 minutes, or until slightly risen in center and jiggly in center when gently shaken. Turn off oven and leave oven door partially open for 30 minutes to allow gentle cooling. Remove from oven and allow to cool completely on a wire rack for 30 minutes before glazing.

To prepare glaze: Preheat oven to 400°F.

Stir sugar and sour cream together and spread on cooled cheesecake. Bake 10 minutes, remove from oven, and cool on a wire rack. Chill cheesecake at least 6 hours before serving. For best results, chill 12 hours or overnight.

Yields 10 to 12 servings.

A Bunch of Layer Cakes and One Fine Cheesecake

"When a band comes to town, one naturally wants to take them to The Grit either for dinner or for the week-end brunch. After that first experience they're hooked!"

—VELENA VEGO, PITCH-A-TENT RECORDS

brunch

Worlds collide every weekend when The Grit serves brunch—customers who stayed up late are served by a crew that got up early, families fresh from church rub elbows with tattooed walking hangovers. Everyone is at their hungriest and the wait can be at its longest. But that primal brunch urge always brings everybody in for their favorite old standbys.

- **Brunch Biscuits Deluxe**
- **45 RPM Pancakes**
- **Super Seven-Spice Potatoes**
- **Breakfast Burrito**
- **Potato Crêpes with Fresh Herb Cheddar Cheese Sauce**
- **Potato and Vegetable Stir-Fry**

Brunch

Brunch Biscuits Deluxe

The Grit makes nearly 500 biscuits on a typical Sunday, but here we present a recipe for a baker's dozen. Even with whole wheat flour in the recipe, the result is tender and delicate . . . but only if the dough is treated gently. Great with **Grit Yeast Gravy**.

> 1-1/2 cups all-purpose flour
> 1/4 cup plus 2 tablespoons whole wheat flour
> 1 tablespoon double-acting baking powder
> 1-3/4 teaspoons sugar
> 1/2 teaspoon plus 2 pinches salt
> 3 tablespoons vegetable shortening
> 2 tablespoons butter, chilled and chopped into small pieces
> 3/4 cup plus 1 tablespoon buttermilk
> 2 tablespoons cider vinegar
> Extremely small pinch of dry mustard

Preheat oven to 450°F. Grease a 10 x 16-inch baking sheet with butter or shortening.

In a large mixing bowl, whisk together flours, baking powder, sugar, and salt. Cut shortening and butter into flour with a pastry blender until particles are extremely fine and well distributed throughout mixture.

Stir together buttermilk, vinegar, and dry mustard. (It is important to note that the pinch of mustard should be extremely small.) Form a well in the flour mixture and pour in the buttermilk mixture all at once. Gently fold in the liquid just until fully combined.

With floured hands, consolidate dough into a ball and transfer to a floured surface. Sprinkle lightly with flour, and pat and flatten dough gently with hands into a slab 1/2- to 2/3-inches thick. Cut into 13 two-inch wide pieces with a floured knife, cookie cutter, or lip of a water glass. Place biscuits on prepared baking sheet with sides just touching.

Bake on middle oven rack 12 minutes or until bottom of biscuits just begin to brown. Remove from oven and brown tops briefly under broiler.

Yields 13 biscuits.

45 rpm Pancakes

These are trouble! The cooks are only supposed to make cakes as big as 45 RPM records, but our brunch fans know better. When they're served, there's a chain reaction in the dinning room and everybody orders pancakes. But there's only so much room on the flat-top!

This recipe is dedicated to the woeful brunch cooks of The Grit. Unlike them, this batter is just as good the following day.

1 cup all-purpose flour	1/4 teaspoon salt
1 cup whole wheat flour	2 large eggs, beaten
2 teaspoons sugar	1/4 cup melted butter
1 teaspoon double-acting baking powder	2 cups buttermilk
1/2 teaspoon baking soda	1/3 cup water
	1 teaspoon pure vanilla extract

Preheat griddle or 10-inch nonstick skillet over medium heat.

In a large mixing bowl, whisk together flours, sugar, baking powder, baking soda, and salt. Stir together eggs, butter, buttermilk, water, and vanilla extract. Stir wet ingredients into dry ingredients just until fully blended. (Batter can be somewhat lumpy. Do not overmix.)

Test the temperature of the griddle or skillet by flicking a few drops of cold water onto it—if drops bounce and sputter, rather than merely steaming or boiling, the griddle is ready for use. Lightly coat the cooking surface with butter or vegetable oil. For each pancake, ladle 1/3 to 1/2 cup batter onto the griddle or skillet from a steady height of 2 to 3 inches. When bubbles first appear on uncooked side, begin checking for proper browning on cooked side. When lightly browned, flip and finish cooking. Serve immediately or keep warm in a preheated 200°F oven while the rest are being cooked.

Yields 6 to 8 seven-inch pancakes.

One-half to 2 cups fresh or frozen sliced fruit or 1 to 1-1/2 cups chopped nuts may be added to the batter. Do not overmix.

Vanilla Iced Coffee

Is this for brunch or dessert? Enjoy it for both, since it's so hard to stop once you start with this stuff.

2 cups double-strength coffee
3 tablespoons sugar
2 tablespoons pancake syrup
3 cups whole milk
Ice

Blend coffee, sugar, and syrup. Add milk and mix well. Serve over ice.

Yields 4 to 6 servings.

"The pancakes are so big you can use them to sleep on, especially good when you have to sleep on someone's hard kitchen floor."

—MAGIC BRIAN,
BINDLESTIFF FAMILY
CIRKUS

Grit Lime-Ade

Who doesn't love an ice-cold, sweet, and tangy drink? Our **Grit Lime-Ade** takes the yin and yang of sweetness and tang to the outer limits with a wallop of fresh lime juice, plenty of sugar, and just enough spring water so that nobody gets hurt.

3 cups spring water, at room
    temperature
1/2 cup plus 2 tablespoons
    sugar
Freshly squeezed juice of 5
    large limes (or enough to
    yield 3/4 cup)
Ice

Blend spring water and sugar. Add lime juice and mix well. Serve over ice.
Yields 2 to 4 servings.

Super Seven-Spice Potatoes

Boil up some tater chunks 'til tender but firm, and sprinkle in **Super Seven-Spice** as you sizzle them in a skillet. It's the recipe for a near-brunch experience!

Super Seven-Spice:
1/4 cup salt
3 tablespoons granulated garlic
2 tablespoons onion powder
2 tablespoons dried parsley
1 tablespoon plus 1-1/2 teaspoon
    paprika
2 teaspoons white pepper
2 teaspoons freshly ground black
    pepper

Potatoes:
1-1/2 pounds boiling potatoes, such
    as round white, round red, or
    Yukon Gold, cut into 1-inch cubes
1 teaspoon salt
2 tablespoons olive oil
Super Seven Spice

To prepare Super Seven-Spice: Thoroughly combine all ingredients; set aside. (Excess can be stored in an airtight container for several months.)

Yields just over 3/4 cup.

To prepare potatoes: Place potatoes and salt in a large pot and add enough cold water to cover by 1 inch. Bring to a boil. Cook 5 to 7 minutes or until tender when pierced with a thin knife. Drain.

    Heat oil in a large nonstick or cast-iron skillet. Add potatoes. Gently flipping with a thin, flat spatula, cook with generous sprinklings of **Super Seven-Spice** until crisp and golden brown. Serve immediately.

Yield 4 to 6 servings.

Breakfast Burrito

A brunch favorite.

4 flour tortillas
4 cups **Black Bean Chili**
1 (15-ounce) batch **Grit-Style Tofu** or 8 large eggs, scrambled
2 cups shredded Monterey Jack cheese
8 tablespoons **Grit Salsa**
8 tablespoons sour cream

Preheat oven to 350°F.
  Wrap tortillas in aluminum foil and warm in oven 15 to 20 minutes.
  Spoon equal amounts of chili and tofu or scrambled eggs down the middle of each warm tortilla. Fold the bottom of the tortilla up 1 inch, then roll it from one side into a cylinder. Cover each burrito with 2 tablespoons **Grit Salsa** and 1/4 cup cheese and place very briefly under the broiler. Top with 2 tablespoons sour cream. Serve immediately.

Yields 4 servings.

Our popular **Border Patrol** substitutes **Grit Pintos** for chili in the above recipe and can be served open-faced with a dollop of sour cream and chopped green onions.

Line Cook Cooler

At The Grit, if the line cooks aren't happy, no one is. But suppose it's the third in a row of swampy, 98° Georgia summer days and your job is to stand for hours between a 400° flat-top and the biggest cheesemelter ever made?
  Ask a cook what he or she wants on a day like that and the answer will likely be "several P.B.R.s"—so sometimes it's better not to ask and just show up with a **Line Cook Cooler**. It has only three ingredients, but the response is always, "Sssssppp! Wow! This was *great!* What *was* this?"

4 cups apple juice
Ice
1 cup spring water
2 lemons, quartered

Fill four glasses with ice and pour 1 cup of apple juice and 1/4 cup water into each. Squeeze 2 lemon quarters into each glass and toss in rinds. Stir and serve with a long straw.

Yields 4 servings.

Brunch

Potato Crêpes with Fresh Herb Cheddar Cheese Sauce

Crêpes:

2 large eggs
1 cup milk
1/2 cup water

1/2 teaspoon salt
1 cup all-purpose flour
3 tablespoons butter

Filling:

8 medium boiling potatoes, such as round white, round red, or Yukon Gold, cut into 1/2-inch cubes
2 broccoli crowns, trimmed and torn or cut into florets
1/3 cup sour cream

1-1/2 teaspoon salt
1 teaspoon freshly ground black pepper
1 medium yellow onion, coarsely chopped
2 cloves fresh garlic, finely minced

Fresh Herb Cheddar Cheese Sauce:

1/2 cup butter
1/3 cup all-purpose flour
3-1/2 cups milk
3 cups shredded cheddar cheese
1 tablespoon chopped fresh parsley or 1 teaspoon dried

1 teaspoon finely minced dill or 1/2 teaspoon dried
3 tablespoons chopped green onions (dark green parts only)
3/4 teaspoon salt
1/2 teaspoon white pepper

To prepare crêpes: Whisk all ingredients together and let stand for 10 minutes. Heat a 12-inch nonstick skillet over medium-high heat. Spray with nonstick spray. Add just enough batter to pan to lightly coat the bottom of pan and swirl pan to coat evenly. Cook until top appears dry and crêpe slides easily in pan, about 45 seconds. Flip or turn and cook until brown spots appear on other side, about 30 seconds. Turn crêpe out onto plate. Repeat with remaining batter, spraying skillet with nonstick spray as needed and stacking crêpes on plate.

To prepare filling: Boil potatoes until barely tender, approximately 15 minutes. Add broccoli and continue cooking 5 minutes. Drain; set aside.

Sauté onion and garlic until translucent. Add to potato and broccoli mixture and stir lightly, add sour cream and combine thoroughly, then mash all lightly together.

Spread about 2 tablespoons of the filling on each crêpe and roll up jelly-roll fashion. Arrange 2 crêpes, seam sides down, on each of 6 plates. Serve with Fresh Herb Cheddar Cheese Sauce.

To prepare Fresh Herb Cheddar Cheese Sauce: Melt butter in a medium saucepan over low heat. Add flour and cook, stirring constantly, for 5 minutes.

Whisk milk into roux, 1/2 cup by 1/2 cup, whisking well after each addition. Cook until thick, whisking constantly. Add cheese and stir until melted. Add herbs and cook over medium heat, stirring frequently, for 5 minutes.

Yields 12 crêpes, enough for 6 servings.

Brunch

Brunch

Potato and Vegetable Stir-Fry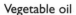

Vegetable oil

2 pounds boiling potatoes, such as round white, round red, or Yukon Gold, peeled and cut into 1/2-inch cubes

Soy sauce

1 cup button or cremini mushrooms, trimmed and thinly sliced

2 carrots, peeled and thinly julienned

1 small head red cabbage, shredded

2 small yellow squashes, quartered and cut into 1/2-inch cubes

2 small zucchini, quartered and cut into 1/2-inch cubes

1/2 green bell pepper, cut into thin strips

1 small or 1/2 large onion, cut into thin crescents

Nutritional yeast

In a large nonstick skillet or wok coated with a minimal amount of vegetable oil, sauté potatoes over high heat until lightly browned, about 5 minutes; set aside. Sprinkle potatoes lightly with soy sauce as they cook.

Stir-fry mushrooms until tender and golden around the edges, about 3 minutes. Add vegetables, pepper, and onion. Using minimal oil and sprinkling lightly with soy sauce, cook until vegetables are crisp-tender and somewhat seared, about 3 minutes.

Return potatoes to skillet or wok and stir to mix with vegetables, then add nutritional yeast to taste and toss to cover completely.

Yields 8 servings.

acknowledgments

An updated edition calls for updated gratitude.

But first we must give serious credit where it is due. Many of the wonderful new recipes we have added are cream-of-the-crop, tip-of-the-iceberg creations of James (Jimmy Ray) Greer, Jeffrey Fox, and Patrick Stubbers. These are the men behind the specials that keep people swarming through the doors of The Grit. Their flavorful innovations include Tofu Wellington, General Chin's 5-Star Tofu Delight, Jimmy Ray's Herbed Dumplings, Roasted Garlic Vinaigrette, Roasted Butternut and Poblano Soup, and Cream of Asparagus Soup, all courtesy of James; Famous Vegan Ranch Dressing, Foxy's Beer Bread, and Thai Coconut Soup, contributed by Mr. Fox; and Citrus Szechuan and Coconut-Ginger Curry Noodle Bowl recipes from Patrick. Vegans with a sweet tooth can praise Grit Renaissance Woman Katie Gasperec for the new dairy-free Carrot Cake recipe.

Now let us blunder into the vast terrain of Special Thanks. We could begin with Jennifer Hartley and Melanie Haner Reynolds for forging a daydream into a place that was ahead of its time and unsurpassed in terms of fond memories. The Grit of today is nothing like The Grit of old; nothing could ever come close. Jennifer and Melanie also deserve thanks for the words they contributed to this edition. Let us thank the many partners mentioned in Melanie's Grit

History (page ix) who passed into and out of The Grit's orbit, especially Jenna Smith Schuh, Jessica's longtime partner before everybody started gettin' hitched and stuff like that. Another whopper would be that guy who bought the crusty old building and kept all the good crust while adding the visionary splendor that inspires as much customer love as the good food. So thank you, Michael Stipe, and may The Grit always do right by the historic landmark that houses it. We hope the friends and fans who gave us glowing blurbs to strew about in this book know how pleased we are with this special aspect of our cookbook. This was largely made possible by the efforts of Velena Vego, our quote-connector and -collector. Thank you, Velena, and of course Miss Barrie Jayne at the 40 Watt Club, for always steering your illustrious guests our way. Carrying over from the first edition are thanks for Regina Quick, Mark Dalling, Larry Tenner, Jason Irvin, and Nicolas Cervini. What a cute little cookbook it has always been . . . thanks to Anne Richmond Boston. We have adored every move she has made as a designer. It is also important to note that any recipes herein that incorporate cashew butter are dedicated to Stephen J. Hurley of Los Angeles, California.

We are especially grateful to all who inhabit The Grit each day: our fine managers, dining room staff, kitchen crew, longtime vendors, and especially our customers (some whom we see more than once a day, some never often enough) and those who have moved on to other places or worlds are missed dearly.

index